PIERRE LOTI AND THE ORIENTAL WOMAN

Pierre Loti and the Oriental Woman

IRENE L. SZYLIOWICZ
Adjunct Assistant Professor
University of Denver

St. Martin's Press   New York

First published in the United States of America in 1988

Printed in Hong Kong

ISBN 0-312-01206-3

Library of Congress Cataloging-in-Publication Data
Szyliowicz, Irene L., 1935–
Pierre Loti and the oriental woman/Irene L. Szyliowicz.
  p. cm.
Bibliography: p.
Includes index.
ISBN 0-312-01206-3: $30.00 (est.)
1. Loti, Pierre, 1850–1923—Relations with women. 2. Loti,
Pierre, 1850–1923—Characters—Women. 3. Women in literature.
4. Exoticism in literature. 5. Orient in literature. 6. Novelists,
French—19th century—Biography. 7. Women—Orient—History—19th
century. I. Title.
PQ2472.Z8S9 1987
843'.8—dc19
[B]   87-12522
                                                                          CIP

To Joe, Michael and Dara

'Pierre Loti'
by Nazim Hikmet

Submission!
Kismet!
Lattice-work, caravanserai
                fountains
a sultan dancing on a silver tray!
Maharajah, rajah
a thousand-year-old shah!
Waving from minarets
clogs made of mother-of-pearl;
women with henna-stained noses
working their looms with their feet.
In the wind, green-turbaned imams
                calling people to prayer;

This
is the Orient and the French poet sees.
This
    is
        the Orient of those books
that come out from the press
at the rate of a million a minute.
But
     yesterday
           today
               or tomorrow
an Orient like this
     never existed
              and never will.

(from *Selected Poems of Nazim Hikmet*, trs.
Taner Baybars, London: Jonathan Cape, 1967)

Contents

1
Literary Overview

At the tip of the Golden Horn, high up on an embankment, looking down on a placid body of water dotted with boats and small craft, sits a small tearoom surrounded by ancient Muslim tombstones. The view from this site is glorious, and the name of the establishment evokes magic and mystery; it is the Pierre Loti Café. Who was Pierre Loti? And why is a Turkish site named after him?

Pierre Loti was the pen-name of Louis Marie Julien Viaud (1850–1923): a sailor, writer, occasional circus performer, adventurer, and member of the Académie française. More than any other turn-of-the-century writer, Viaud/Loti brought the unfamiliar to France; wherever he travelled throughout his extensive maritime career, he recorded his sensations, his impressions, and his emotions, and he transmuted these experiences into both fictional and non-fictional works. Many of the places he visited – Tahiti, Japan, Turkey, Senegal, parts of South-east Asia, and countries in the Middle East – provided him with domiciles over a period of time ranging from several weeks to several years. He attempted to learn the languages and immerse himself in the culture of the various countries he visited.

As a result of Loti's exposure to the 'Orient' (an all-encompassing term for these exotic lands), the Occidental world in general became more familiar with a large and hitherto mysterious part of the world. As a Frenchman and product of the nineteenth-century colonialist mentality, he exhibited certain contemporary prejudices but, by and large, he was more objective than most European observers and genuinely tried to appreciate the culture and people of the countries he visited.

Loti's popularity was enormous during his lifetime, but it has suffered considerably ever since. Two main reasons exist for this decline. The first is the topical character of his subject-matter – the exotic lands which so fascinated the European armchair-traveller have become more easily accessible since his death; the second is that Loti's literary manner has become dated. The sentimental

1

treatment of his heroes and heroines, the somewhat simplistic characterisations, the excessive indulgence in subjectivity ('le culte du moi'), the *fin-de-siècle* morbidity and despair, and the romantic attachment to nostalgia and the longing for a simpler age are all typical of the period in which he wrote. In the following era, the simple sailors and their faithful wives, the primitive Orientals and their exotic surroundings no longer satisfied the cravings of a more sophisticated literary élite nurtured on the works of writers such as Gide, Proust, Claudel, and Sartre. If Loti's reputation has declined and if the literature he wrote is no longer read,[1] why then should we study this author? Is his present literary status deserved? Or was his previous popularity a more correct assessment of his artistic merit? In examining this author's life and work, I hope to provide some answers to these questions.

Probably one of Loti's most engaging characteristics was his candour and his willingness to share his experiences – both public and private – with his readers. He was particularly frank about his liaisons with women; everywhere he travelled he found female companions with whom he established relationships, and his feelings toward these Oriental women provided much of the interest in his 'Oriental' novels. Since the sailor/writer led his audience to believe that his descriptions of places were realistic, he also led them to believe that his portrayals of the female indigenes were accurate. Given the stereotypical quality of all the women depicted regardless of cultural variations, it seems pertinent to enquire why all these Orientals were invested with a certain sameness and why Loti's fictional representations of Oriental women should exhibit similar tendencies. The answer is that they lead to the glorification of the European hero or his real-life counterpart. Clearly whatever formula the French author had discovered for appealing to his countrymen must have had some basis in his characterisations, for apart from the Breton novels and the many non-fiction travel books, the 'Oriental' novels were very much in demand and were certainly one of the reasons for his election to the Académie française.

Over the past decade in particular, scholarship in feminism and feminist issues has alerted readers to sexual bias in the formulation of women's roles in society and to the codification of these stereotypes in literary texts. As men define gender and its symbolic importance, they have consigned 'woman' to a subordinate position; she has been variously viewed as

Other,[2] as Pygmalion-formed passive creation,[3] as chattel ('thingified'),[4] as 'exchange',[5] as 'dehumanized sexual possession and . . . status symbol',[6] and as 'projection of the female aspect of the male psyche'.[7]

Feminist studies rebel against the masculine use of women as instruments for self-aggrandisement and/or self-fulfilment and protest the treatment of women as chattels. They condemn relationships where mutual interaction is irrelevant or avoided and where sexual satisfaction becomes an end – for men. Finally, they refuse to sanction feminine self-definition in masculine terms or acknowledge that 'her [woman's] existence lies in man'. Instead, what must be addressed is 'why woman should be defined with relation to men'.[8]

In addition to invoking problems of self-definition, feminists view male/female relations in political/ideological terms as a struggle for power and sexual dominion,[9] thus radically revising our accepted notions of heterosexual inter-relationships. Whether discussing English literature,[10] French literature,[11] or American literature,[12] feminist studies have provided a re-vision of our outlook on male/female attitudes and relations in life and, in its natural extension, art.[13]

Although feminine literary perspectives have been confined, to date, to the study of Occidental civilisations, the position of women in Oriental societies is also under scrutiny. Historians and social scientists are demonstrating that the traditional portrayal of women in these societies has been biased and based on Western judgements. European ethnocentrism and male chauvinism have combined to account for this phenomenon. The traditional Occidental attitudes of scholars and observers of the East were invested with feelings of inherent superiority, and 'objective' scholarship was frequently tainted by these implicit beliefs.[14] Oriental women, in particular, have been viewed conventionally by Westerners as innocent primitives,[15] uncorrupted by civilisation. They have been regarded as lacking autonomy and requiring protection from the superior, worldly, sophisticated, preferably Western, man. Since these women were regarded as ignorant and artless, they could be manipulated easily by their dominating masters, and further, this masculine paradigm presented these women, like their Occidental sisters, as actually craving male domination.[16] Certainly France's sailor/author subscribed to many of the then current conventional attitudes toward women; how they were incorporated into his 'Oriental' texts will be the subject of this enquiry.

Loti's attitude towards Oriental women is particularly worthy of study for several reasons. Although some critical work relevant to this topic is available, no detailed study has yet been prepared. In fact, those scholars who do deal with this problem have come to radically different conclusions. Typical of one viewpoint is the statement by Raymonde Lefèvre: 'Loti embodied the cult of feminism. He not only loved *some* women, he loved *woman*.'[17] Another conclusion, one espoused by Rolande Leguillon, a more recent critic, finds that 'women exist [in Loti's work] only to the extent to which they serve to draw out the masculine personality'.[18] Can these two views be reconciled? And if not, which one is more valid?

Loti's interest in the Orient influenced his total oeuvre, and his treatment of women was a significant element in his works. By comprehending the Oriental/Occidental, male/female dynamics, I hope to gain new insights into the Loti oeuvre. In such a study many questions arise. Was Loti's attitude characteristic of that of nineteenth-century Frenchmen? What was the position of European women in the late nineteenth or early twentieth centuries, and was this different from or similar to that of Oriental women at that time? How did the fictional female protagonists reflect this reality? What was the role of Oriental women in his literary accomplishments? Did his attitude toward these women change over time? If so, why? Since Loti was a pre-eminently autobiographical writer, what do his fictional postures reveal to the reader about the author? Finally, what can we learn about Loti and his work from examining his stance towards Oriental women? To what conclusions can one come regarding the man, both as individual and as literary figure? In order to explore questions such as these, I shall survey the imaginative or fictional oeuvre, concentrating upon the 'Oriental' works (*Le Mariage de Loti*, *Aziyadé*, *Le Roman d'un spahi*, *Fleurs d'ennui*, *Madame Chrysanthème*, *La Troisième Jeunesse de Mme Prune*, *Fantôme d'orient*, and *Les Désenchantées*). Relationships with women play a dominant role in all these novels.

A critical problem that has always confronted a Loti student is the confusion between Loti the author and Loti the hero of his books. As most of his works are by and large autobiographical, the events depicted and the relationships portrayed lead the reader to assume that the fictional and the actual are identical. Loti himself carefully fostered this image by displaying Aziyadé's stela and discussing in his strictly autobiographical works (*Le Roman d'un enfant, Prime Jeunesse,* and *Un jeune officier pauvre*) many of the same events he fictionalises. As a result, readers were led to believe that he was a womaniser and that the feelings he ascribed to his novelistic protagonists were accounts of his actual sentiments *vis-à-vis* the women portrayed.

Early biographers tended to accept this view, although there were notable exceptions even during Viaud's lifetime. Henry James, in a chapter entitled 'Pierre Loti', in *Essays in London and Elsewhere,* voiced his suspicions concerning Loti's authenticity when he stated: 'We have a great and I think a just dislike to the egotistic–erotic, to literary confidences on such points, and when a gentleman abounds in them the last thing we take him for is a real man of action.'[19] Camille Doucet opposed the sailor/writer's candidacy for the Académie française on the grounds that 'He made himself the perpetrator of imbecilic legends behind which I find no one.'[20] N. Serban, Loti's earliest biographer, maintained that, although Loti was exceedingly open in sharing many of his momentary and more ephemeral feelings and thoughts with his readers, he carefully hid from them those aspects of his life which he considered important and which he wished to remain private.[21] These views of Loti were in the minority. Most critics tended to accept his self-portrait at face value and described his life and its important events according to the manner in which Loti presented them.

In recent years, however, the critical view of Loti has changed dramatically and most scholars no longer accept the traditional interpretation. Two of his most recent English critics both agree that Loti's diaries contain a wilfully created image. And, in fact, Clive Wake's entire thesis in *The Novels of Pierre Loti* rests on the contention that the novelist was actually a homosexual who perpetrated a heterosexual myth upon his reading public.[22] While Michael Lerner in *Pierre Loti* does not emphasise the Frenchman's homosexuality, he finds that

he created his own cult of himself in his writing using a retrospective cult of his own experiences and a romanticizing cult of people and places derived from his reading and masochistic personal relations . . . so as to conceal from himself and others his insecurity and childish real self.[23]

Not only did Loti disguise himself from his audience, but he succeeded in creating a fanciful view of the exotic lands he visited and then depicted in his fiction. A year after the Wake and Lerner books were published, a French-educated Turkish woman argued in her thesis that Loti's vision of the Orient was one of his own creation: 'In fact Loti's Orient is not the Orient of the Orientals, but the make-believe through the real.'[24]

Whether Loti was indeed a dissembler is a critical question, the answer to which will inevitably affect any analysis of his works. In my view, the authors cited above provide ample evidence to conclude that one must treat Loti's writings with caution. Loti himself lent credence to the position that he was not always as candid as he appeared to be when he said in a letter to his friend Emile Pouvillon, dated 1 April 1881, that another friend had remarked

> that there are several different layers in me, deposited by the abnormal circumstances in which I have had to live, and that the *moi* which is at the bottom, the real one, is a primitive man, a species of prehistoric savage, who reveals himself from time to time and scares people.[25]

Thus, his self-portraits (or those of his fictional *alter egos*) may or may not mirror the 'real' Loti, even though the French author clearly wished his public to accept the fictional portrayal as authentic.

Once the reader begins to suspect the author's veracity, other questions come to the fore. If he is untrustworthy in portraying himself, how reliable can we find his expression of sentiments towards other people? And if his views become suspect, how can one find the *real* Loti? And if we set aside his stated ideas, what can we deduce from his writing that will provide insights into his actual attitudes – in this instance, his attitudes towards Oriental women?

Such questions cannot be answered easily by reference to existing scholarship for, to date, there have been very few analytic treatments of Loti's works. Most of Loti's biographers concentrate on one aspect of his personality or one perspective found in his works – pessimism, *fin-de-siècle* ennui, exoticism and primitivism, artistic (painting) interest, orientalism, romanticism, escapism, or dealings with women – but few of these studies have gone beyond describing the biographical 'facts' of the author's life and summarising the plots and themes of his works.

The Lerner and Wake books cited above are the most analytical treatments in English of the Loti oeuvre and they provide us with original scholarship. Wake's psychoanalytic approach affords new insights into Loti's probable homosexual tendencies and concentrates on his close relationships with various sailor friends who appear in different guises in his novels. Wake further maintains that some of the love affairs may be seen as fictional representations of Loti's attractions toward these men. Lerner's study contributes a more general overview of the entire Loti canon and discusses the various works in chronological order from a biographical perspective, setting Loti in the 'moral context' of the time. He emphasises Loti's 'individuality' and 'contemporaneity' and he succeeds admirably in acquainting the general reader with his works.

Of the other studies in English none is really first rate. Edmund d'Auvergne's 1926 work, *Pierre Loti: The Romance of a Great Writer*, offers a eulogy to a personal friend, but gives few insights into the man or his work. D'Auvergne was apparently taken in by the fictive author and accepted everything Loti wrote about himself as truth. Lesley Blanch's recently published *Pierre Loti: The Legendary Romantic* is disappointing because the author seems unaware of the most recent scholarship, and, like d'Auvergne, is completely deceived by Loti's self-created personality. Hence Blanch is unable to evaluate Loti's work impartially. Her thesis is that 'he [Loti] did indeed live those exotic episodes and many more, pretty much as he recounted them. His life was such that he had no need to invent.'[26] Some newly released photographs as well as a few bits of gossip about the mistresses and women friends with whom Loti surrounded himself during his final years reveal some hitherto undisclosed information, but the literary aspects of the French author's life are treated in a breathlessly worshipful and uncritical manner.

Two doctoral dissertations in English have been written on Loti: Alexis J. Richards's 'Exoticism in the Works of Pierre Loti' (State University of Iowa, 1949) and Robert Brown Johnson's 'A

Reexamination and Revaluation of the Dual Nature in the Life and Work of Pierre Loti' (University of Wisconsin, 1949). Richards provides a valuable background by compiling a history of 'exotic' literature starting with the first books written about the extraordinary, the unnatural, the love of the strange, and the desire for new sensations, but she contributes few insights into Loti's work. Moreover, the extensive descriptions of plot and theme are critically useless.

Johnson's dissertation examines Loti's pessimism and unsuccessful search for faith and argues that Loti's vision derives from a deeply pessimistic nature. Emphasising the influence of Loti's conservative convictions on his writing, Johnson argues that the Frenchman was basically immoral and he refuses to excuse his behaviour: 'His egotistical worship of pleasure demanded complete independence from moral codes.'[27] Moreover, he alludes tangentially to Loti's relations with women and does so in an original manner. Although he does not treat the topic in detail, he is the only writer in English to perceive Loti's relationships with women as that of master/slave and he further contends that Loti was often tyrannical and cruel toward his mistresses.

The body of French scholarship on Loti is, naturally, much more extensive, but here, too, few publications are noteworthy. One of the best and earliest is that of N. Serban, cited above, one of the most comprehensive and balanced biographies extant. Although he knew his subject, he was not charmed (as others have been) into writing a laudatory and subjective work. He argues that throughout his life, Loti was pursued by nostalgia and a fear of death, and it was the memory of good times or an imaginative vision of happiness (which he associated with the Orient) that consoled and comforted him. In addition, he maintains that the lure of the exotic and the oriental were the basis of all Loti's interests. What attracted him to remote and colourful places were 'the dreams associated with their far-off origins. "The Oriental coast of Africa", "the Indian Ocean", "the Polynesian Islands", these names evoked for him visions of sun, blue sky, a complete phantasmagorical mirage.'[28]

In contrast, Pierre Flottes, in *Le Drame intérieur de Pierre Loti*, contends that the lure of the Orient was less significant for Loti than the influence of specific experiences in exotic lands. He attempts a psychological interpretation of Loti's actions and writings but is not as insightful as Clive Wake. Raymonde Lefêvre also provides psychological insights in *La Vie inquiète de Pierre Loti*; in *Le Mariage de Loti* and *Les Désenchantées de Pierre Loti* she contributes the most detailed analyses of two of his major works. In her biographical study she attempts to understand why a common sailor might resort to writing. Her thesis is that Loti 'was tormented by the need, not only to translate his feelings, but to communicate them to others, in order to try to make them last, to tear from nothingness the memory of what he had known, loved, suffered'.[29] She maintains, in a generally approbatory portrait, that the Protestant ethic with which Loti was imbued caused him a great deal of guilt in his relationships and that writing was one means of overcoming this. She isolates the themes he deals with as those of 'fear of aging, of death, and terror of nothingness'.[30]

Another biographer who examines Loti 'the man' in order to understand Loti 'the novelist' is Helen Scribner. In *Pierre Loti vu à travers son oeuvre* the author presents a thorough study of Loti's attitudes towards every aspect of his life and examines in detail the author's complex nature. She contends that his sensuality affected all his relationships and ideas, and ultimately she faults him for being too narcissistic. Judging him against the Christian ideal of individual renunciation for the common good, she concludes that Loti was an immoral individualist, but she excuses his non-conformist behaviour by blaming it on a physical impediment: 'neurasthénie'.[31] Her analyses and thorough examinations are more useful than her conclusions which now appear dated.

Whereas Scribner tries to examine Loti from many different perspectives, several other biographers have isolated one aspect of the writer and have attempted to establish that one as the definitive clue to his work. Among these are C. W. Bird in *Pierre Loti: correspondant et dessinateur, 1872–1889* and Keith G. Millward in *L'Oeuvre de Pierre Loti et l'esprit fin de siècle*. The former reports that Loti's artistic skills included his ability to paint and draw and argues that his keen sense of observation was first sharpened through sketches he made on his first trips. The latter examines the *fin-de-siècle* spirit of the period and shows how it permeated Loti's works. Millward sees Loti as being feminine in his inclinations – a product of the turn-of-the-century mentality.[32] Odette Valence and Samuel Loti-Viaud (Loti's son) in *La Famille de Pierre Loti ou l'education passionnée* discuss Loti's early years and his relations with his family. They ultimately perceive Loti's oeuvre as an outgrowth of his youthful experiences and they view him as strongly influenced by his family relationships.

Family and early life experiences aside, Loti biographers also tend to place their subject in the context of his travels. Among the more valuable studies in this tradition is Pierre Briquet's *Pierre Loti et l'Orient* which summarises the literary activity dealing with the Orient prior to Pierre Loti's writings and then places his books in that tradition. In addition, this exhaustive study details the influence of the Orient on Loti's style through words, language, and decor. It is, however, limited in scope, for Briquet considers the Orient and Turkophilia to be synonymous and deals only with those Loti works that possess a Middle Eastern theme.

For interesting insights into Loti's attitudes toward Africa and the Africans, Léon Fanoudh-Siefer's *Le Mythe du nègre et de l'Afrique noire dans la littérature française* faults Loti for generalising from a particular experience, thus creating an inaccurate impression of Africa and formulating an African myth: 'While periodically indicating that the action takes place in Senegal, Loti extends the texture of his impressions first to the whole Sudan, then to Nubia, to Africa in general, and finally to the entire black race.'[33] Not only is Loti ill-equipped to deal with Africa as an entirety on the basis of his limited experience, but Fanoudh-Siefer complains that the sailor/author's vision is marred by his subjective, Occidental perspective:

> This writer looked at the land of Africa in projecting on it his morbid and unhealthy inner feelings, his personal, climactic obsessions. For him everything is sad, unwholesome, presaging death and bad luck; all is mysterious, bizarre, strange, illogical and impure.[34]

Another significant work that concentrates on Loti's Oriental myth-making, but this time from a Turkish perspective, Thérèse Fallah-Najmeh's 'La Femme musulmane vue par Pierre Loti', focuses on Loti's relationships with the Turkish women depicted in *Aziyadé*, *Fantôme d'Orient* and *Les Désenchantées*. She accuses Loti of not fully understanding the Turkish women he portrayed even though he was knowledgeable about the role of Muslim women in Turkish society.[35] Moreover, she criticises Loti (as well as all Occidental men) for being attracted only to the mysterious, sensual and romantic Middle East, rather than to its actuality. She also sees his attraction to Oriental women as part of his attraction for the Orient; since anything Oriental affects him favourably, so, too, would the women there. As corroboration of this view, she cites a passage from the *Journal intime* which states: 'Everything which touches upon Islam either closely or from afar attracts me and exercises its charm upon me.'[36] She is sceptical of Loti's real reasons for loving the Oriental women he describes, and affirms that his ego, rather than the Oriental woman, is being immortalised.

Her analysis leads her to conclusions very different from those reached by Basil Rafter in *La Femme dans l'oeuvre de Pierre Loti*. Whereas Fallah-Najmeh deals exclusively with the Muslim (that is, Turkish) experience, Basil Rafter focuses on the woman in general, including the Occidental woman. Much of his discussion concerns the influence on Loti of various female members of his family. Rafter sees Loti's attitude towards women as positive due to the Viaud/Texier close family relationships and the special rôle young Julien occupied in the household. Furthermore, unlike Johnson, cited above, he defends Loti's hedonism and sensuousness by saying that despite these, 'Loti retained toward the female an attitude which, even though it was implied or even unconscious, was no less strong and was intimately connected with his childhood.'[37]

This brief review of the existing literature on Loti suggests four distinct conclusions:

1. The critical writing in both French and English is limited and its quality is very uneven. Some of it tends to be impressionistic and only a few works are analytical.

2. Loti's disarming candour leads one to believe that his autobiographical approach reveals an accurate portrayal of the author. In fact, however, several critics find the self-portrait suspect, which leads to questions regarding the authenticity of his attitudes in general.

3. Much of the literature tries to relate his biography to his fiction; it discusses the literature in terms of Loti's life rather than treating the fiction as an independent entity.

4. Although several books deal tangentially with Loti's feelings towards women and two studies address themselves specifically to the issue, no student of Loti's works has analysed his treatment of Oriental women from a feminist perspective.

By and large the Occidental women portrayed in Loti's novels fall into generally conventional categories of loyal, strong wife, mother, and grandmother concerned with carrying on the tradition of the nuclear family despite all adversity (for example, *Pêcheur d'Islande* and *Mon Frère Yves*; Cora in *Le Roman d'un spahi* is a notable exception). Although they are frequently abandoned by their sailor husbands, either because the latter's careers force them to be away from home or because the sea has finally claimed them, the women survive through strength of character and force of love. In the case of the Oriental or exotic women, the reader observes a different mould. They are simple, primitive, dependent, often helpless, and they appear to worship the hero as though he were God. They, too, are faithful and adoring, and would like to continue a relationship which, in each instance, the hero terminates. After their conquest by the Occidental man, however, they are unable to live. Only in *Les Désenchantées*, an early feminist tract unlike any of Loti's other novels (and one which will be discussed in Chapter 6) do we find another stance, and even here, the heroines die. This treatment of Oriental women cannot be analysed apart from Loti's portrayal of the civilisations of which they are a part. Although Loti tended to be more accepting of foreign civilisations than many of his fellow countrymen and less willing to judge them as inferior, except in the case of Japan, a country he thoroughly disliked, it is important to consider the extent to which his portrayal of the social contexts which his feminine characters inhabited were accurate.

After all, Loti was still a product of his Occidental milieu, and thus of the prejudices with which he was raised. He prided himself on his 'objectivity' toward the various lands which he visited and, by extension, their inhabitants, but his attitudes were none the less influenced by traditional Western views of the Orient. For this reason I feel it is necessary to examine not only the author and his works, but the actual societal situation about which he wrote.

Accordingly, I shall first discuss Loti's biography since this is crucial to his work. The three autobiographical works – *Le Roman d'un enfant, Prime Jeunesse,* and *Un jeune officier pauvre* – will provide some of the material for both the facts of his life and his views on women, but secondary sources will provide some insights and information that Loti omits.

In Chapter 3 I shall examine nineteenth-century attitudes toward women, both in Europe (where Loti was raised and thus culturally influenced) and in the various countries he visited. This will provide a basis for an understanding of the degree to which Loti's portrayal of Oriental women is consonant with social realities.

Chapter 4 will examine the extent to which traditional interpretations of Loti's attitudes toward women are borne out by our readings of the Oriental oeuvre. How does Loti treat women in the various novels in this canon, and what conclusions can be drawn from an analysis of these works? And how were his actual experiences transmuted into literary ones? What was the relationship between his observations of the society and his portrayal of indigenous women? And finally, to what extent can one apply psychological insights to Loti's depictions based on the earlier discussion of his life and his thought?

Although France's sailor/writer was convinced that his relationships with women were based on mutual admiration and understanding, I perceive him as an exploiter of women, ready to use them to satisfy his various needs. Further, Loti formed these associations in order better to understand the people and cultures of the different countries in which he lived. Were the fictional portrayals in fact accurate representations of the societies in question, and particularly of the women therein? Did the social and political conditions exist as Loti saw and described them or were his descriptions tinged by preconceived notions or romantic illusions? These women became the instruments by which he could gain a more penetrating perception of the area, and when he had to depart, he severed his emotional attachment with little thought of the consequences for his mistresses, their unhappiness and suffering. Moreover, Loti frequently used women to mask a homosexual relationship or to draw attention away from an unsavoury liaison. In addition, women supplied Loti with the necessary self-confidence and ego-satisfying emotions to enable him to promote his own self-image to his readers. Chapter 5 will explore Loti's needs and the various means by which he manipulated the women with whom he lived.

Finally, Chapter 6 deals with the way in which women used Loti, for *Les Désenchantées* describes a real-life relationship which Loti experienced and then transcribed fictionally. The whole incident, however, had been arranged for his benefit by a Frenchwoman who was visiting two non-Turkish friends when Loti arrived in Constantinople. Sensing that he exploited women they decided to take their revenge and set in motion a series of meetings and 'adventures' between the famous Frenchman and themselves. They pretended that they were Turkish women who were oppressed by their cultural conditions, and enticed him into believing that he alone could be a spokesman for their plight, and that only he could proselytise to the West on their behalf. Loti created his final novel to proclaim their cause.

Through the examination of the various 'Oriental' works and the author's views contained therein, we shall learn whether Loti was characteristic of his time or was a unique voice, and whether his attitudes towards the Oriental woman were one of the great attractions of his prose. Finally, with our feminist sensitivity we will test our reactions to the relationships described in the novels to see whether they continue to affect us as they did our predecessors. After all, the greatest test of art is its universal appeal over time. Through the medium of the Oriental woman we will try to determine whether or not Loti's work can stand the test of the future.

2
The Role of Women in Loti's Life

Loti's life and his writings are intimately connected. His fiction and non-fiction are based on actual experience, and his extensive use of the first person heightens the autobiographical quality of his work. From the time he was very young he kept a diary, and the notes he made or the actual entries he recorded served as the basis for most of his published work. On the whole, his style is impressionistic: he recorded feelings about experiences as they occurred, and he either embroidered upon them or transferred them *in toto* to the new text. Sometimes entire passages were transcribed directly from the journal into his novels, with very little revision.[1] As a result, Loti's fiction has a striking feel of immediacy. He skilfully evoked the atmosphere of the places he describes. Bathing exotic spots in a spirit of nostalgia, he prompted romantic associations that proved most appealing to his readers.

Loti's 'foreign' fiction is almost formulaic: in each instance a handsome, usually French, sailor travels to a distant land, there to fascinate, and in turn be enthralled by, an 'Oriental' woman. The charm of this relationship and the allure of the seductive female provide the intrigue of the novel and these features, along with their exotic setting, were primarily responsible for the popularity of his books. Since women are such key elements in all the 'exotic' fiction, it is necessary, when considering his life, to focus on his relationships with women and the ways they influenced his thought.

Viaud's writing talent sprang from inauspicious surroundings. His father, Jean Théodore Viaud, was a bureaucrat in Rochefort, a small French town on the Atlantic coast near La Rochelle, about 300 miles southwest of Paris. Here he met and married Nadine Texier, a young woman of Huguenot ancestry, who came from the Isle of Oleron at the mouth of the Charente near La Rochelle. The elder Viaud, like his father-in-law, had converted from Catholicism to the strict Calvinism of his wife's religion. Julien

Viaud's religious background and his mother's intense piety were to be major influences throughout his life.

Julien was born on 14 January 1850, 19 years after his sister, Marie, and 12 years after his brother, Gustave. The household was dominated by women; in addition to the immediate family, it contained his two grandmothers, his great-aunt Clarisse and her aunt Rosalie, both of whom were to appear later in fictional settings as Tante Claire and Tante Berthe in *Le Roman d'un enfant*. His father seems to have exerted little or no influence upon him[2] and his brother left home to train as a surgeon when Julien was eight. The man who would later be known as Loti grew up as a much-loved, spoiled little boy,[3] indulged by his mother, his sister, and his many live-in relatives. His earliest memories seem to revolve around these women and the affection they lavished upon him, and his greatest fear was that they would leave him and that he would then be alone.

> They told me later that when I was quite small, I never permitted anyone from the family to leave the house, even for the slightest reason or visit, without ensuring their intention really was to return. 'You will come back again, won't you?' was a question which I was accustomed to ask anxiously after having followed those who were going out to the door.[4]

Above all, it was his mother to whom he turned for protection and love, not only as a child, but throughout his life. He speaks of her as a 'shelter', a 'refuge' against 'fears of the unknown', as 'supreme protection' and 'a nest of nests'. He associates his earliest fears with her departure and his anxiety that she might not return. Long after he reached adulthood and had already had his first love affairs, he continued to praise her and indicated that he preferred her to other women. He speaks of her as 'my mother who is still the most precious and most stable, who is still the one to whom I cling with the tender confidence of a small child, when terror of destruction and nothingness seizes me'.[5]

Both Nadine and her daughter, Marie, seem to have possessed some writing skill, as published letters of their correspondence attest, and Théodore himself wrote poetry, plays, and a history of Rochefort. Thus it appears that Julien inherited his artistic ability and sensibilities from both sides of the family.

Viaud's childhood seems to have been quite happy. He was

loved and protected by his family members, but apparently made few friends. He was particularly close to the daughter of some family friends, Lucie (Lucette) Duplais, who was a few years older than he, and he played with her frequently on the estate of La Limoise, about three miles from Rochefort.[6] When he was seven, he lived next door to a little girl named Antoinette, born in 'the colonies', and her life-style and the exotica which filled her house greatly attracted him.

Interestingly, Julien mentions several little girls with whom he became acquainted over the years, but except for a youngster named André whom he befriended in school,[7] there is little mention of his male friends until he became a sailor. Then, however, during different stages of his life, he met several men who were to affect him profoundly.[8]

Of the men Julien knew, his brother, Gustave, was clearly the greatest single male influence on his formative years. 'My brother . . . my intimate and secret counsellor',[9] was the way the mature author would describe him in *Prime Jeunesse*. Gustave was away or abroad during a good portion of Julien's youth, but his search for the exotic and his vocation of naval surgeon affected his younger brother deeply. His impact on the youngster was reinforced by the many letters sent home from the exotic locales he visited, and by Nadine Viaud's constant references to her missing son.

> For fear that the absent member of the family should be forgotten even for a moment, she constantly brought the conversation round to him or her, making doubly sure by producing 'relics', as the family called them, objects of clothing, favourite possessions, anything at all which would remind them of the absent one.[10]

As a result, although the brothers were together infrequently, it is universally acknowledged that the younger man so admired and respected Gustave that he tried to emulate him.[11]

On the eve of his departure for Tahiti, Gustave presented Julien with a copy of *Voyage en Polynésie*, a picture-book of Tahitian life, which became the younger boy's favourite book during his early youth. He was particularly impressed with the picture of an attractive, bronzed woman crowned with reeds who was identified as 'S. M. Pomaré IV, queen of Tahiti'. (Loti was to meet her years later and be present at her death.) The beautiful brown Tahitian ladies he saw in his picture book inspired him to paint them again and again, but he turned them into white and rosy-skinned Caucasians. 'I made them white, oh! white and pink . . . I found them ravishing that way.'[12] He was quick to acknowledge, however, that all children are influenced by their culture in their aesthetic assessments, and that these assessments might change later in life, especially when influenced by their senses.[13]

The exotic locale evoked by the book coupled with the many descriptions of Gustave's Tahitian family stimulated the young brother's imagination and his desire to visit Oceania some day. The letters Gustave sent from Tahiti kept the image of an exotic spot in the forefront of Julien's imagination, and it is therefore not surprising that this island furnished the setting for young Viaud's first foreign adventure.

Loti's attitudes were probably profoundly shaped by the nature of his early educational experiences. Until the first years of his adolescence, Julien was privately tutored, as the family was afraid that he was too delicate for normal schooling. When he was 11 years old, his parents enrolled him at the Collège de Rochefort, now the Lycée Pierre Loti. Here he attended classes with children his own age, but since he had been accustomed to solitude and over-protection, he did not feel privileged by the new experiences. On the contrary, he was a misfit socially and rebelled against the discipline necessary to maintain good grades.

Julien was not a good student and hated his studies. Lucette, his sister Marie, and Aunt Claire all supervised his education and made sure his homework was done, but this was no easy task. Time and again he informs his readers that he hated school work and did his best to avoid it.[14] Later on he was to say that school days left him with 'impressions which, still today, are painful and depressing for me whenever I think about them'.[15] Perhaps his lack of interest in academics and intellectual endeavours prompted him to select simple, unschooled, unintellectual women with whom to form relationships.

He disliked academic subjects; his favourite classes were painting and music in which he always did well. He was quite a good artist and originally considered becoming a painter rather than a writer. Some of his sketches have been published.[16] Otherwise he was an uneven student at best, first in some subjects and last in others. His best work came in translation and at the end of each year he always received a prize for his achievement in this area.

He was an independent spirit – he liked to write, but not for school. Assigned themes repelled him and he received his worst grades in 'la narration française'. But from an early age he loved to bury himself in a tiny old office connected to his museum (which contained specimens of butterflies and shells) where he would work on his journal. 'Already I had the need to note down, to fix passing images, *to struggle against the fragility of things and of myself,* which have caused me to stick to this journal up until these last years.'[17] Initially he wrote in code so no one could read his entries, but gradually he reverted to regular script, although he kept the manuscript under lock and key.

His career objectives underwent several changes. Then and later, young Viaud was obsessed by his future and the kind of respectable career toward which he could aspire. His fear was that he would be mired '*in a given place, in a circumscribed spot* and then grow old and this would be all'.[18] Influenced by the religious atmosphere in his home, he initially (at seven or eight years of age) thought about becoming a pastor. His love of the exotic prevailed, however, and he soon declared missionary work to be his goal. Thus he felt he could combine his religion with a search for adventure. But as he matured, his faith became more tenuous and he realised that it would be impossible for him to embark upon a religious vocation. At this point he no longer had any definite career ambitions, so his brother, who was concerned about his future, wrote to suggest that, because of his facility in mathematics and a 'certain preciseness of mind', he considered engineering as a proper avenue for his talents. The youngster's response was lukewarm: 'It's all the same to me.'[19] Nevertheless, because of Gustave's interest, the family considered enrolling Julien in the Ecole Polytechnique.

It was during these uncertain times that Julien felt desperate and overwhelmed by life; he expressed his desire to remain a child and never grow up, a desire he was to reiterate frequently throughout his life. His nostalgia for the past, his fear of change, and his conservative stances were almost an obsession; he feared any disruption in family life or any change in routine. Even the thought that his mother's workbox might undergo wear and tear horrified him, much less the idea that his mother might change or die.

The idea that I could know a time when these much-loved hands which touch these things daily will never again touch them is a horrible thought against which I feel I have no courage . . . This, mother's workbox, and these dresser drawers, these, no doubt, are what I will abandon with the most melancholy and worry when I will have to leave this world.[20]

If we may credit the first volume of his autobiography, *Le Roman d'un enfant*, which was published in 1890, Loti's general attitudes seem to have been formulated early. His excessive love for his mother deeply influenced all aspects of his life, especially his feelings about religion. All his life he wished for faith but was unable to reconcile his experiences and thoughts with an abstract theology. His inability to believe in any religion inspired extreme guilt because of his mother's strong beliefs and her disappointment that he did not share her religious convictions. Many of her surviving letters counsel her son and plead with him to believe. His novel *Aziyadé* transposes this struggle into fiction by presenting several letters from Loti's sister which urge him to act in a Christian manner. He responds with missives which speak to his feelings about religion:

The idea of Christianity remained wavering in my imagination for a long time, even when I no longer believed in it; it had a vague and consoling charm. Today its glamour has fallen absolutely. I know nothing so vain, so untrue, so inadmissible.[21]

Nevertheless, he continued to search for faith; *Jérusalem, La Galilée,* and *Le Désert* chronicle his quest in the Holy Land, but it is his secular rather than his spiritual experiences there which make the voyage memorable for him.

Still another problem with which Julien wrestled was that of his sexuality. At the Collège de Rochefort, Julien made friends with only two boys, André and Paul, but unlike them, Viaud had never made a sexual conquest. The subject of their hastily scribbled notes was always girls. His immaturity was evidenced by his need to match their experiences. The 'love' which he claimed was actually Jeanne, an old family friend rather than a sexual conquest.

Julien informs us in his autobiography that, from an early age, he loved to dominate women. When he was twelve he was sent to visit some cousins in the mountains during summer vacation. The two little girls with whom he stayed were aged ten and eleven. He played with them daily and they became close friends, but he fancied himself their superior, both in age and intellect, and loved being their chief. After a few unsuccessful 'revolts' by Titi, the elder, he was declared uncontested head of the group, and he revelled in his domination. This would set a pattern for his future associations: 'Later, for my amusement, I had many others, less easy to lead; but always I preferred them to consist of people younger than I, above all when they were younger in spirit, simpler, neither controlling my fantasies nor ever smiling at my childishness.'[22]

At fourteen he used to dream of a woman whom he identified with youth and love. He thought of 'her' again and again, and her presence filled him with 'immense melancholy' and her 'immense mystery with its supremely sad charm' remained with him for a long time.[23] In *Le Livre de la pitié et de la mort* she becomes more tangible. He describes her as 'very young, creole, bare-headed with black curls arranged around her forehead in an old-fashioned manner; with beautiful, limpid eyes, seeming to want to speak to me, with a mixture of sad bewilderment and childish candour; perhaps not absolutely beautiful, but possessing supreme charm . . .'.[24] Just as he is about to reach her, he awakens and the dream disappears.

His first sexual encounter, however, was not with a 'creole', but with a bronzed, dark-haired gypsy, whose deep-coloured eyes seemed to hide 'all the sensual mysticism of India'.[25] After five or six days of being bewitched and bothered by explicit sexual dreams, he seduced her (or was it the reverse?) in the middle of a jungle-like ravine, a place in which the entangled natural configurations seemed to symbolise his confused emotional state. Although France's future sailor/author never referred to this experience again in his works, his first sexual encounter seems to have influenced him profoundly – all of the women he memorialised in his Oriental works had the same primitive, forthright, almost audacious quality.

Throughout his life Loti was obsessed with physical beauty. All of his heroines were attractive, often beautiful creatures, for beauty was very important to him and he hated ugliness. 'It is the physical appearance of these women – this "charming envelope" of which Loti will speak later that is a necessary given for the women he loves.'[26] In an era when Balzac, Flaubert, and Zola were popular, Loti still retained the traditional notions associated with chivalrous and pastoral romances. All his heroes are magnificently handsome; his heroines are beautiful, graceful, and sexually appealing. This is true for both the Oriental and the Occidental characters he portrays. The Oriental women, however, are all endowed with additional 'virtues', passivity and a simple belief in the perfection of their Occidental paramour (usually Loti). They conform to the European stereotype which equated the Orient and the women it produced with 'sexual promise . . . untiring sensuality, unlimited desire, [and] deep generative energies'.[27] Each Loti novel finds the protagonist's needs and desires being met by the individual or individuals selected by the hero to act out his fantasies. In only one instance, *Le Roman d'un spahi*, is the hero disappointed in love – and then he recovers to find a young woman servilely awaiting his every pleasure. Interestingly, his *Journal intime* announces an unsuccessful love affair, but does not signal any subsequent relationship with an indigenous mistress. As usual, Loti's imagination projects the male figure as captive to the woman's intense desire for him.

His concern with physical appearances extended to his personal relationships as well. He associated with good-looking sailors and all his heroes were attractive men. Clive Wake terms Loti's concern with physical appearance an 'obsession' and interprets Julien's reliance upon handsome sailor friends as a subconscious need for brother-substitutes. He finds the 'frère-marin' relationship legitimising the sexual implications of filial attraction.[28] This concern with human beauty may stem from Loti's acute awareness of his small stature as well as his perceived unattractiveness. He possessed an inferiority complex in this regard; as Wake notes:

> A sentence from his unpublished diary . . . dated June 1869, indicates his preoccupation with his lack of physical beauty. Referring to himself by the pseudonym he used during this period, he writes: 'Fédin contempla au grand jour son corps repoussant et ses longues pattes.' ['Fédin contemplated his repulsive body and his long paws in broad daylight.'][29]

Julien blamed his parents for his underdeveloped physique – they had never forced him to exercise. He tried to remedy this deficiency in later years; he spent seven months in Joinville near

Paris in 1876, participating in a physical training course 'to possess the beauty I do not have'.[30] His wish to appear attractive led him to dress up in dandified clothing. Loti's penchant for high heels, perfume, make-up, jewellery, and elegant dress extended beyond the fancy-dress parties he loved; he often wore 'accessories of feminine gear' in order to recapture 'the fugitive illusion of youth'.[31] He particularly enjoyed the masked balls and costume galas then currently in vogue. In addition, he loved to play tricks on friends and acquaintances, disguise himself when on shore leave, and generally act as prankster.

> One knows all the tales of this academician who loved to ring doorbells and then hide, who loved to appear incognito, who came to visit in a sailor's costume. 'We spoke of him,' wrote Léon Daudet, 'as putting on a mask in order to buy a croissant.'[32]

Although such actions are not necessarily indicative of deviant sexual behaviour, ample proof exists that Loti was bisexual.[33] One biographer in particular maintains that Viaud's homosexual tendencies can be traced to Gustave's sudden death on a ship in the Bay of Bengal in 1865 when Julien was fifteen.[34] His death and its unusual circumstances (burial at sea) certainly affected the youth. He also wanted to sail over the spot in the Bay of Bengal where his brother was buried, so he could feel some tangible contact with Gustave.

Young Viaud's decision to enter the navy showed his independence from his parents, who had discussed this career as a possibility amongst themselves. They had indicated that they would never consent to sending their youngest child into the navy, partly because they were reluctant to separate more than one son from the family hearth. Julien, however, revolted against his parents' stand: 'precisely upon hearing what [my mother] had just said to me: 'We will keep you!' I understood for the first time in my life the whole project already scarcely consciously formed in my head, of going away also, of going away even further than my brother had, anywhere, across the whole world'.[35]

Julien's naval career was precipitated by both Gustave's death and his father's disgrace. Théodore Viaud was accused of embezzlement in 1866, and the family attempt to replace the missing 14,000 francs in bonds caused the Viauds to fall deeply into debt. Théodore lost his job on 2 June and was imprisoned briefly thereafter; the family dishonour was almost too much for Loti to bear. The sale of the family house at Rochefort was an ever-constant threat and part of the author's motivation to write and earn money was to prevent such a calamity. The elder Viaud was, in fact, fully exonerated in February 1868, but by then the many debts he had incurred forced Julien to leave home and enter a career of which his parents would have disapproved under other circumstances.

In October 1868 he left for Paris and entered the Lycée Henri IV. His experiences in Paris were mainly unhappy ones; he was homesick and lonely, and it was here that he began the 'journaux intimes' that would eventually number 200 volumes. These diaries are of singular importance for understanding Loti, for they not only chronicle his impressions and emotions but also serve as a basis for all his published work, and we shall see later the correlation between Viaud's life as he recorded it and the subsequent transmutation into fiction.

After a fairly dismal year, Julien passed his examinations in July 1869, and received his first commission on board the vessel *Borda* in October of that year. The two years he spent attached to this ship were for the most part unhappy. He was lonely, homesick, and frequently hospitalised for illnesses such as mumps and sore throats, but there is real reason to believe that part of his problems were psychosomatic.[36] In addition, he was disappointed that his first tour of duty was largely stationary; the ship was anchored in Brest most of the time, so his dreams of sunny climes and exotic locales were unrealised.

In October 1869 Julien was transferred to the *Jean Bart*, and here he finally began his world-wide wanderings. He was still 19 and had been promoted to second-class midshipman. His first tour of duty took him to the Mediterranean, touching at ports in southern Europe and North Africa, and then sailing to New York and Nova Scotia. When the ship returned to France, the sailors were informed that the Franco-Prussian War had begun, so the various crew members were transferred to different vessels to fight in the war. The young sailor was assigned to the *Decrès* to participate in the blockade of the Baltic Sea and Heligoland. This experience was not what he had anticipated when he joined the navy; the dreary life and bad weather did not appeal to him. Nonetheless, he would later draw on these experiences to create *Pêcheur d'Islande*.

In June 1870 Théodore Viaud died, and his youngest son was left with the responsibility of supporting his mother and aunts. Henceforth, all his trips would be punctuated by return visits to Rochefort to see his family. Even after his mother died, he continued to return home, where he established a curious Oriental atmosphere by decorating several rooms with exotic furnishings.

When the war ended in 1871, he joined the *Vaudreuil*, which set off for South America and the Pacific in May of that year. In *Un jeune officier pauvre* he describes some of his adventures on this voyage. *Fleurs d'ennui* and *Figures et choses qui passaient* both contain stories based on these experiences. From Valparaiso he was transferred to the frigate *Flore* which sailed to Tahiti, the land of which he had dreamed for so many years. Although he only spent two months here (January to March and between 26 June to 4 July 1872), he would later, in *Le Mariage de Loti*, transpose his memories into a stay which lasted over a year. The various characters are all based on actual people Julien knew, but their names were changed 'presumably for purposes of aesthetic distancing'.[37] Loti would follow this technique throughout his oeuvre: he would experience an adventure or a situation, embellish it, and then filter it over time to suppress its negative aspects and enhance the positive ones in the author's (or his protagonist's) favour.

Although *Aziyadé*, his novel about his later Turkish exploit, was published first (1879), *Le Mariage de Loti* appeared in 1881; it dealt ostensibly with his love affair with a particular Tahitian woman, Rarahu, whom he loved and then left. In fact, however, she was a composite character. Julien wrote in a letter dated 24 February 1879 that 'the truth is respected only in its details, the base of the story is not true: I combined several real people to make one only: Rarahu, and that seemed to me a pretty faithful study of the young Maori woman'.[38] It was on Tahiti that Viaud changed his name to Pierre Loti – Loti was the name of a flower peculiar to the South Seas island; and his Maori girl friends named him that because 'Viaud' was too difficult for them to pronounce. One of them, named Rarahu, pronounced 'Loti' over and over again, as proof of her love for him.[39] Julien chose the first name 'Pierre' for himself apparently because he admired an ancestor, Pierre Viaud, who had been a courageous naval captain, although it has also been suggested that he took this name during the period of a close friendship with Pierre Le Cor, a fellow sailor.[40]

Tahiti and Loti's experiences there made a profound impression on him. His station in life at the time (a newly appointed officer), a new-found recognition of himself, and his susceptibility to sensations and strong emotions contributed to his feeling of freedom. In addition, the Polynesian mores permitted him to enjoy sensuality to its limits, freed from the constraints of European society and civilisation. 'He went from the simple life of a scarcely emancipated high school student, to the remarkable ripening of an exceptionally voluptuous and excitable nature; he lived in a kind of frenetic and sensual repose, an intense accumulation of virile power.'[41] Julien himself acknowledged the strength of his sensuality and its impact upon him to his good friend, Joseph Bernard, a fellow sailor, in a letter dated June 1874: 'I cannot resist my passions, and all follies are possible for me.'[42] However, he softened the negative impression that such a statement might make by conceding a feeling of guilt, probably due to lingering effects of his religious background: 'At least I am not completely corrupted, because I cry afterwards, and I am afraid of evil.'[43] The remorse never lasted long, however, and he was always willing to continue a relationship until he tired of it – or until the ship left for another port.

Loti left Tahiti in July 1872, and the notes he made in his *Journal intime*, as well as the articles he published in *L'Illustration* (August 1872 and September–October of the following year), along with some sketches he made, helped him to recreate the experience six years after it happened. The Rarahu adventure took place in 1872, but the novel was written in late 1878 and early 1879, and quickly accepted by Calmann-Lévy, his official publisher. Simultaneously, Mme Juliette Adam, editor of *La Nouvelle Revue* and the author's 'intellectual mother',[44] serialised the work in the January and February 1880 issues of her magazine under the name of *Rarahu*.[45]

At the same time as he was writing the book which was to become *Le Mariage de Loti*, he met Sarah Bernhardt, with whom he established a life-long friendship. The actress was also an eccentric, keeping a skeleton named Lazare in her rooms along with a vampire bat in a black satin-hung room containing a white satin-lined coffin, in which she sometimes reclined. Loti had tried repeatedly to meet 'La Divine' but had always been unsuccessful.

Finally, after many unanswered letters and an attempt to dedicate *Aziyadé* to her, which arrived too late for the publishers to include in the finished work, he resorted to a ruse. He dressed up as a Japanese in elaborate dress and make-up in the hopes that he would gain her attention. She continued to ignore him and sent him away. He then decided to try another stratagem, to introduce himself to her à la Cleopatra – rolled up in his gift, a handsome Persian carpet. This time he was successful:

> Loti finally crashed the gates by having himself rolled up in a magnificent Persian carpet and delivered by two stalwart Arabs as a gift to be laid at the feet of the lady. The Arabs unrolled the heavy cocoon, Loti half smothered emerged, Sarah screamed with laughter, and after that the author of *Madame Chrysanthème* was a regular guest.[46]

From then until their final meeting in 1922 when she came to visit him in Rochefort, the two artists remained good friends. To memorialise their friendship, he dedicated *Le Mariage de Loti* to her.

Meanwhile, when Viaud returned from the Pacific to Europe he was involved in several assignments, and in June 1873 went back to Rochefort for a three-month stay with his family. While there, he was promoted to sub-lieutenant, and discovered that his closest friend at that time, Joseph Bernard, was being sent to West Africa. Through high-placed connections, Julien managed to embark for Senegal as a passenger. From November 1873 to May 1874 he lived in Dakar and travelled extensively between that city and Saint-Louis, the old colonial capital of the country. During the last months of his stay he experienced his most intense and passionate love affair – with the wife of a local trader. She was French and in June 1874 she accompanied her husband back to France. Several of the relevant pages in the *Journal intime* are missing, so details of the affair are unclear, but we do know that Viaud sailed back to France the following month in order to find her. We also know that he went to her home in Annecy and that she elected to stay with her husband. The circumstances of this visit are surrounded by mystery, as are the author's reactions in his diary, but the Senegalese experience and his feelings for 'la française' were translated into the fictional Cora of *Le Roman d'un spahi* (published 1881).

Like his previous work, the novel is by and large autobiographical. It was the first publication to bear his pseudonym: Pierre Loti. All the characters were based on people Viaud had met, and the names of two of them, Jean Peyral and Julien Julia, were lifted from actual people he knew, although the fictional personages were not identical with their real-life counterparts. This African adventure represented a revolt against his Puritan upbringing and is notable in that it chronicles both the deep passion and the profound disgust Loti experienced when he confronted his sensuality.

The year 1874 was one of crisis for Loti: his unhappiness with the outcome of his love affair was matched by his feelings on learning that Joseph Bernard had resigned from the navy. He was so deeply affected by these two events that he requested a transfer to the naval physical training college at Joinville. Here he fell dangerously ill in February 1875 of a fever, and he was extremely sick for one month. Even after his recovery, he suffered from depression and nightmares for a long time.

The Joinville stay was followed by a brief stint as a clown in a local circus in the spring of 1876, and then Loti received his orders for Salonica and Constantinople. He was stationed in Constantinople from late July 1876 until March 1877, first on board the *Couronne* and then on board the *Gladiateur*. He began writing about his adventures almost as soon as he returned to France, encouraged by a naval friend, Lucien Jousselin (the Plumkett of *Aziyadé*.) *Aziyadé* was completed early in 1878 and published the following January. Although this work recounted his third 'exotic' adventure, its story and details were the most recent and vivid, and the novel became his first publication.

From 1877 to 1883, Loti's chief naval assignments were in Europe, except for a brief one-month cruise in the Mediterranean, during which he stopped at ports in North Africa (the experiences would later be transmuted to *Fleurs d'ennui*). This was a relatively peaceful period; he freed the family of its debts and saw to it that the Rochefort house was restored to his mother, lodger-free; he became a familiar figure in Parisian salons, and he continued to cement his friendship with Mme Adam. During this time he briefly entered a Trappist monastery (1879) but he left the following month, disillusioned and suicidal. He seems to have been very bored with his life and with himself – he was lonely, felt unloved, and was plagued with guilt about his lack of faith and his homosexual tendencies. This was also the period when Julien was particularly close to Pierre Le Cor, a fellow sailor who would become the model for Yves Kermadec in *Mon Frère Yves*. Although Loti had met Pierre in 1867, a decade passed before they became really good friends. Le Cor was married and an alcoholic, and Loti apparently viewed himself as father-figure and self-appointed rescuer for the young sailor who suffered constant bouts of drunkenness. As with all the officer's close male friends, Le Cor's body also attracted him.

> When Pierre removes his clothes, one would think he were a Greek statue removing his coarse exterior, and one admires him. – In the same bronzed alabaster, hard and polished, are outlined the mobile bulges of his muscles and the powerful lines of an ancient athlete.[47]

The books published during the 1877–83 period reflect Loti's obsession with exotic lands and the women he encountered there: *Aziyadé* (1879), *Le Mariage de Loti* (1880), *Le Roman d'un spahi* (1881), and *Fleurs d'ennui* (1883). 1883 also saw the publication of *Mon Frère Yves*, Loti's testament of friendship to his frequently intoxicated companion, Pierre Le Cor. It was initially serialised in the *Revue des deux mondes* (August and September) and marked the beginning of his most productive period. He published extensively, almost a book a year, both novels and travel literature.

In 1883 he met Oirda – Mme Lee-Childe, a cultivated Parisian aristocrat, who was very impressed with his writing. Their initial relationship was epistolary, but she finally came to Rochefort to visit him.

> Through Oirda's guidance and tact, Loti was steered through the labyrinths of Parisian social life. She saw him clearly, and knew just how to help the secretly timid provincial to overcome his sense of inferiority among the critical Parisians. . . . Through the taste of this luxurious woman, who was also a connoisseur, Loti was to develop his own sense of luxury, and his passion for acquiring *objets d'art* [author's italics] with an expert's eye.[48]

Unfortunately, Oirda died four years after they first met, but Loti commemorated his friendship with her by dedicating *Propos d'exil*, the first of several travel books and essays describing exotic lands and Loti's reactions to them, to her memory. That book and *Mon Frère Yves*, appeared in the *Revue des deux mondes* (1884–5). The next books alternated in subject-matter between novels with a Breton or an Oriental theme and travel essays dealing with his trips to the Orient (mostly the Middle East but with a few excursions into China, Japan, India, and South-east Asia). In addition, Loti wrote four plays between 1893 and 1911, two of which, *Pêcheur d'Islande* (1893) and *Ramuntcho* (1908), were based on earlier novels of the same name.

Madame Chrysanthème, a novel/reminiscence was set in Japan and published in 1888. *Japoneries d'automne* appeared the following year, a book about Japan which belongs in the travel essay category. *Le Roman d'un enfant* (1890) is an autobiographical work based on his earliest years. In the same year, *Au Maroc*, a travel essay describing his trip to Morocco and his reactions to the country and its people, was published. *Le Livre de la pitié et de la mort* (1891) is a collection of short stories, and *Fantôme d'orient* (1892), a semi-novel, recounts the author's adventures as he returned to Turkey to find Aziyadé. In 1893 both *Matelot*, a Breton novel, and *L'Exilée*, an account of Loti's visit to Carmen Silva, the Romanian queen in exile in Venice, appeared. *Le Désert* (1895), *Jérusalem* (1895), and *La Galilée* (1896) find the sailor/author questing for his symbolic roots and his faith in the Holy Land. Finally, *Ramuntcho*, a novel set in the Basque country, was published in 1897.

During these years, Pierre Loti continued his maritime career and married Jeanne Blanche Franc de Ferrière in October 1886. Part of the reason he seems to have travelled so much during this time was because he was married unhappily.

It is noticeable, for example, that he spends his first wedding anniversary searching for Aziyadé in Istanbul, is about to leave for Morocco when his son is born, and spends most of the next decade or more in the Middle East and Asia. And even when he was in France he was only occasionally seen with his wife.[49]

Blanche assumed the rôle of mother and mistress of the house, but his heterosexual needs seem to have been fulfilled by Crucita Gainza, a young Basque woman, who was imported from her homeland to be installed in a modest house in Rochefort.

When Loti chose to settle this second ménage at Rochefort rather than anywhere else, where anonymity might be preserved, it told of his indifference to public opinion in his home town, and to the distress it would cause his wife – to say nothing of his mother, though perhaps, ostrich-like, he thought this new life could be concealed from *her* at least [author's italics].[50]

Not only does this speak of 'indifference to public opinion', but it also indicates an insensitivity to feelings and needs of those close to him. This egocentric attitude towards life and toward others is flagrantly displayed in his art.

Viaud's liaisons were marked by a singular lack of responsibility – both in his life and as transmitted into fiction. In the 'Oriental' novels the fictional closure is often death – with the hero leaving his beloved and the young lady dying of a 'broken heart'. In actuality, Julien was too self-involved ever to form a reciprocal relationship with any woman. He was concerned always with the impression he made on others and the power he exercised over them. Again and again he made statements such as: 'My career as a sailor and my long voyages exert their prestige on all these people; the question becomes who will be my friend, who will be my mistress.'[51] This dichotomy expressed itself in his sexual attitude toward women: he viewed them as serving either a sensual or an intellectual purpose; no woman could serve both. 'The women with whom he shared the transports of the flesh were not expected to have intellects, or to make conversation. Their bodies communicated sufficiently.'[52] Those women like Juliette Adam and Oirda were valued for their friendship and their sensitivity as well as their minds, and the French author was careful to retain them in a non-sexual relationship.

Despite his mercurial personality, he seems to have had a gift for retaining friends, and he apparently had many of them from all walks of life. He prided himself on his association with his sailor buddies and boasted that 'the companions that I chose for myself have, it is true, participated in every career, and navigated under all flags . . . They are a handful of men whom I hold in my hand and who are ready to follow me even into fire'.[53] Although he had many friends in the aristocracy or upper classes, he always preferred the companionship of those inferior in position to him, whether on ship or on land, and this was equally true of his relationships with either sex.

One other woman played a significant rôle in his life: Berthe Durutty, wife of Etienne Durutty, the Basque physician who was a very close friend of Loti and with whom he shared many adventures. Berthe was childless, and although Loti seems to have tempted her to become his mistress on many occasions, she remained faithful to her husband. However, she adored the author and carried on a long epistolary love affair with him, addressing him in terms of endearment in the Basque language. Some of her remaining correspondence provided Lesley Blanch with the occasion to inquire into the reasons for Loti's magnetism for women. She concludes:

> A packet of these old letters remained at Hendaye [Loti's home in the Basque country] stuffed in a cupboard, where they had escaped the bonfire to which Loti, at the end of his life, consigned such outpourings. When I looked through them, with that painful feeling of eavesdropping which is known to every biographer, I wondered once again – what was this curious power which Loti could exercise over so many women? To be famous was not enough. He was egocentric, and no Adonis. I put the question to a very old lady at Hendaye, who nudging a hundred, was still elegant, and perfectly able to recall Loti, whom she had known well. 'Those eyes – he could make you his slave with those eyes,' she told me . . . 'He knew all about you, he noticed everything you wore, too . . . and then, those eyes of his *undressed* you!' [Author's italics][54]

Despite his several woman friends, Loti's favourite female companion remained his mother, and until her death in 1896 at the age of 86, he spent as much time as possible at Rochefort so that she would not be alone. By and large he was considered something of an eccentric, so his handsome sailor friends, his make-up, and his dandified clothing were tolerated – even in provincial Rochefort. When he was not in his home town or sailing on the high seas, he spent time in Paris attending balls and frequenting the literary scene. As a result of the many friends he made there, he was elected to the Académie française on 21 May 1891, defeating Emile Zola in the campaign to replace Oscar Feuillet.

After 1897, the bulk of Loti's publications consisted of travel literature and political writings, although he published one novel, *Les Désenchantées* (1906), one autobiography, *Prime Jeunesse* (1919), and one novel/reminiscence, *La Troisième Jeunesse de Mme Prune* (1919). In addition, *Figures et choses qui passaient* appeared (1898), a collection of reminiscences, stories, and impressions of diverse places. From 1899 his writing became more polemical; even when he described his travels and the interesting spots he visited, he wanted the reader to sympathise with him as he mourned the passing of great civilisations and deplored the onslaught of modern technology which, he insisted, would ruin the new societies being formed. Whether he was in China (*Les Derniers Jours de Pékin*, 1902), in India (*L'Inde sans les anglais*, 1903), in Iran (*Vers Ispahan*, 1904), in Egypt (*La Mort de Philae*, 1908), in Spain (*Le Château de la belle au bois dormant*, 1910) or in Cambodia (*Un Pèlerin d'Angkor*, 1912), Loti trumpeted the same theme: new inventions and less traditional ways are the scourge of ancient, great civilisations and cause their decay and finally, their ruin. He has seen it again and again (Angkor Wat, Luxor, China's Imperial City): all give testimony of the passage of great societies. Wherever he travels he seeks past greatness, and he is always disillusioned by the present-day decadence. This motif is evident in his fiction as well – according to Loti, Tahiti and Turkey suffer from the incursion of modernity, and the prostitution in Oceania and the various excesses noted in the Ottoman Empire are symbols for the decline of traditional society. Japan was particularly offensive to him, for he viewed that society as totally modern – meaning that it was unnatural and artificial. He predicted the 'Yellow Peril'[55] and a warmongering future for that country.

In 1905 Loti returned to France from Turkey and his involvement with the three ladies who would star in *Les Désenchantées*. Although he was in poor health, he was put in command of the Fourth Maritime Depot at Rochefort until 1906; later that year he was promoted to the rank of captain, a position he retained until his retirement from the navy on 14 January 1910. The remaining 13 years of his life were devoted to travel (mainly in Turkey), a stint in the military (he volunteered for duty in World War I in August 1914) and writing – primarily polemics defending Turkey and the Turk from negative European attitudes toward both the country and its inhabitants. *Suprêmes Visions d'orient* (1913), *Turquie agonisante* (1913), and *La Mort de notre chère France en orient* (1920) all deal with this topic. In addition, he composed vigorous tracts protesting against Germany: *La Hyène enragée* (1916), *Quelques aspects du vertige mondial* (1917), and *L'Horreur allemande* (1918). After the war, Loti's son, Samuel Viaud, collaborated with his father to write the autobiographies *Prime Jeunesse* (1919) and *Un jeune officier pauvre* (published posthumously in 1923).

Pierre Loti had been ailing for a number of years, but he had always fought courageously for his principles – both by writing and by fulfilling many non-combat missions in the French military. Regardless of the unpopularity of his stance, Loti refused to abandon it just because it was out of favour. Even though Turkey was officially an enemy of France, he continued to publicly praise the country. As he hated Germany and the Germans, he tried to induce the French to negotiate with the Turks in behind-the-scenes diplomacy in order to persuade the Turks to ally themselves with the French. He was very disappointed that his diplomatic efforts were unsuccessful. His campaign to proselytise on behalf of what he perceived to be the oppressed Turkish woman also occupied his writings.

His last years were spent in failing health, working with Samuel Viaud on the Loti journals in order to write the three autobiographies. In typically egocentric fashion, he devoted many hours to preparing his last wishes – deciding on the contents of his will and the disposition of his remains. Loti died on 10 June 1923, after years of deteriorating health. He was given a state funeral and then buried in accordance with his wishes in the garden of his ancestors' home in Oleron. Although Loti's life was spent travelling all over the world, in death he chose to remain in his favourite land, France.

3
Nineteenth-Century Attitudes towards Women

I EXOTICISM

The search for the exotic generates a rich tradition in French literature, a tradition which can be traced back at least to the chroniclers of the Crusades, such as the *Mémoires* of Villehardouin (1212), and which achieves its most luxuriant growth in the nineteenth century. The interest in foreign lands and strange societies manifests itself in two literary genres: travel literature which was essentially 'objective' reportage, such as Tavernier's *Voyage en Turquie, en Perse et aux Indes* (1676) and Bernier's *Voyages* (1699); and fantasy travel, for example, Rabelais' *Pantagruel* (1532), Montesquieu's *Lettres persanes* (1721), Diderot's *Supplément au Voyage de Bougainville* (1722), Abbé Prévost's *Manon Lescaut* (1731), and Bernardin de St Pierre's *Paul et Virginie* (1788). Pierre Loti works in both genres and finds his most characteristic modes of expression in them.

Exoticism exercises several different forms of appeal. Some writers seek to escape the incursion of industrialisation,[1] others, reacting against naturalism, seek out the exotic as the appropriate stuff of 'melancholy idylls in dream-like settings'.[2] A third group is composed of members who are dissatisfied with their squalid, urban environments and imagine that a retreat to simplicity and 'natural' surroundings will provide the happiness which they find so elusive.[3] Among these are the sensualists who use artificial stimulants to transport themselves into an imaginative universe where their desires may be satisfied and their senses gratified.[4] The reality of the locale is often a matter of little concern; the 'exotic' is associated with escape – usually from a bourgeois, conformist, and materialistic environment.[5]

Of all the fascinating, exciting, and intriguing landscapes available to the French imagination, none has been more alluring than the Orient – the Orient as a vague, mythic ideal associated with danger, strange customs, and vaguely perverse sexuality. In the nineteenth century, serious academic studies by philologists, archaeologists, and students of Near and Middle Eastern culture, spurred on by Napoleon's invasion of Egypt, combined with the interest of artists and writers who found the Ottoman Empire a fertile field for imaginative adventure. These two approaches to a specific type of exoticism coalesced into a distinct intellectual perspective – that of Orientalism.

II   ORIENTALISM

According to Edward Said, 'Orientalism' assumes both an academic interest in any aspect of study dealing with the Orient, 'a style of thought based upon an ontological and epistemological distinction made between "the Orient" and (most of the time) "the Occident" ' and 'a Western style for dominating, restructuring, and having authority over the Orient'.[6] In short, Said's argument revolves around the Western domestication of the Orient – the translation, for Occidental consumption, of Oriental ideas, thought, and values by Western scholars, travellers, diplomats, and imaginative writers. Necessarily, this translation is, in effect, an interpretation based upon the values the 'Orientalist' brings to bear on his experiences – values rooted in his home culture. In the nineteenth century the findings of the Orientalist, expressed as truths, were accepted as received wisdom, and much future scholarship and many popular attitudes were based on their conclusions.[7]

According to these Orientalists, Europe represented strength, the Orient, weakness. 'The Oriental [was] irrational, depraved (fallen), childlike, 'different', thus the European [was] rational, virtuous, mature, "normal".'[8] Europe was familiar; the Orient was exotic, mysterious, profound, and seminal.[9] The Orient eventually became both more and less than a specific geographic area; it became, particularly for Romantic imaginative writers, a mythic idea, encompassing a complex of emotions and symbols, many of which had little to do with Oriental reality.

This was certainly true of Islam. Unlike the fictive Orient, which 'was primarily a source of aesthetic inspiration for Romanticism, Islam was, for a small number of French Romantics, above all, a matter of spiritual and moral concern'.[10] The lure of the exotic, the mystery of the undiscovered or the newly rediscovered, led these artists to perceive Oriental culture through the prism of imagination. Thus Islam was seen not as a true civilisation, but as a springboard for testing literary sensibilities. Islam fascinated these artists for symbolic reasons; the culture – its mysterious otherness – inspired literary reactions unobtainable from Occidental associations.

The exotic encompassed not only the Islamic world but ancient empires and legendary lands. Although Praz singles out Gautier and Flaubert as artists whose 'dreams carry them to an atmosphere of barbaric and Oriental antiquity, where all the most unbridled desires can be indulged and the cruellest fantasies can take concrete form',[11] they were by no means the only ones to project their suppressed needs on to the Orient. Throughout the nineteenth century, starting with Chateaubriand and Lamartine and including Fromentin, Maxime du Camp, Baudelaire, Rimbaud, Nerval, and Loti, most of the great French writers quested for happiness and peace of mind in the Orient or some exotic land (for example, America) and found their objective unattainable.

Many of the books written about far-away places were situated in the colonies, and a whole new literary *genre* emerged – that of 'colonial literature'. According to Lebel, this literature includes fiction or non-fiction written either by tourists or by local inhabitants. Many of these observers had only a superficial knowledge of conditions, and wrote of their limited experiences and impressions 'not absolutely to create a true work, a colonial work, but rather to entertain the public, and toward that end it [was] necessary to represent the country as exotically as possible'.[12] Thus, picturesque descriptions, couched in clichés, regardless of geographic, sociological, or physical accuracy, impressed the uninitiated. These fantasies perpetuated the myth of the exotic.

This phenomenon applied to sexual preconceptions as well.[13] The Orient symbolised a type of licentious sexual experience that titillated the European imagination. Many of the late nineteenth- and early twentieth-century authors searched for erotic sensations outside the confines of their staid, European upbringing.

What they looked for often – correctly, I think – was a different type of sexuality, perhaps more libertine and less guilt-ridden; but even that quest, if repeated by enough people, could (and did) become as regulated and uniform as learning itself. In time 'Oriental sex' was as standard a commodity as any other available in the mass culture, with the result that readers and writers could have it if they wished without necessarily going to the Orient.[14]

Not only was 'Oriental sex' a 'standard commodity', but its concept was specifically masculine. In this exclusively male domain, women were always treated as products of a male power-fantasy: 'they express[ed] unlimited sensuality, they [were] more or less stupid, and above all they [were] willing'.[15] Furthermore, the liaisons were never permanent, for the Occidental considered himself superior to his Oriental paramour, and this was equally true of homosexual associations.

How does Loti fit into this Orientalist paradigm? How does his fictive vision differ from (or conform to) reality? Is his view of the exotic a representation of the real world or an imaginative interpretation based on Romantic fantasies? In order to answer such questions, it is necessary to discuss the status of women in the various countries in which Loti set his 'Oriental' novels – Tahiti, Senegal, Turkey, and Japan. By giving a short overview of the culture and mores of these countries at that time, we can better determine whether Loti accurately described the society he saw and whether he understood the social dynamics operating within it (specifically among its women) or whether he imposed an 'Orientalist' viewpoint on his Occidental readers in order to appeal to their imaginations and further perpetuate the stereotype.

Loti's judgements were clearly rooted in a nineteenth-century Occidental (French) perspective. Accordingly, it is also necessary to explore the position of women in nineteenth-century French society, the culture in which Julien Viaud was raised. Thus we can better determine whether his fictional female creations reflected his own culture or whether they expressed only the impressions he received of his host countries.

III FRANCE

Jean-Jacques Rousseau was one of the first French writers to enunciate the proper role for French women when he stated:

The entire education of women must be dependent on men. To please them, to be useful to them or make themselves loved and honoured by them, to bring them up when they are young, care for them when they are older, counsel them, console them, render their life agreeable and pleasant: these are the duties of women at all times. As long as one doesn't steer away from this principle, one will not swerve from the goal.[16]

The 'goal' was domestic education, and this point of view was supported by other French intellectuals.

Joseph de Maistre said: 'Knowledge is what is most dangerous to women.' Proudhon could see only two possible roles for them, housekeepers or prostitutes, and rated their intellectual and moral value as one-third of that of men. Michelet . . . wrote in praise of them but only to extol them in their traditional domestic role.[17]

Various men, including Montesquieu, Helvetius, Condorcet, and Saint-Simon had advocated equality in education, politics (suffrage), and marriage reform, but by and large, conservative views prevailed throughout the nineteenth century and into the early twentieth century. Thus, it is not surprising that it was not until 1935 that full equality was accepted by the CGT, France's labour union.

The prevalent literary attitude towards women found a correlative in the legal status of women. Women were treated as legal minors.

Normally marriage involved community of property, but not community in the management of it. The husband had the sole right to administer the joint estate: he could alienate her personal property, though he could only enjoy the usufruct of her real estate. Even in marriages with separation of property the wife could not alienate her own real estate without her husband's consent. Even if the wife obtained a separation from her husband, she still needed her husband's signature for all her business affairs; all she gained was the right to live where she pleased, with whom she pleased but she could not sell her property.[18]

The Napoleonic Code (1804) succeeded in divesting

Frenchwomen of all the rights they had gained during the French Revolution.[19] It protected the man rather than the woman, by permitting him every indulgence of his passions without concomitant punishment. Young girls up to the age of 13 were shielded; after that, they were on their own.[20] Fathers were not responsible for their illegitimate children; young girls after the age of 11 who were seduced or 'defiled' were unprotected 'provided violence was not used'. Fathers were not penalised for engaging in 'traffic of [their] daughter's virtue', nor were husbands punished for open adultery.[21] By and large, marriage was a financial contract undertaken to improve the position of the partners: 'the husband seeks a dowry and the woman buys at once a protector and a manager considered more experienced for the administration of her property'.[22] This presumed the woman's inability to handle her estate. The same mentality discouraged women from thinking and from becoming educated. In 1884 there were still 3,281 communes without primary schools for girls and 31.34 per cent fewer girls' schools than boys' schools in France.[23]

In French working class circles, man was expected to be the breadwinner while woman was regarded as housewife or 'angel of the hearth'. Only in extreme instances of poverty or economic necessity would a woman seek additional income for the family. Men were seen as workers, women as their companions. French labour leaders used this situation to contend that women were exploited 'victims' of a capitalist conspiracy, but they defended women for propaganda purposes, and not because they were intrinsically interested in their welfare.[24] Under these circumstances, one would expect to find Frenchwomen downtrodden, submissive, and fully controlled by men. This, however, was not the case.

Despite economic exploitation, philosophical opposition, and legal inferiority, Frenchwomen exerted a powerful influence in the nineteenth century, and, according to Violet Stuart Wortley writing in 1908, were more influential than Englishwomen at that time.[25] From 1791, when the first French feminist, Olympe de Gouges, issued her Declaration of the Rights of Women, until 1944 when women obtained the vote, French feminism had many allies, but unlike the English movement, it favoured moderation. The more moderate French stance was due partly to the high percentage of females in the work force,[26] partly to the strong Catholic influence in the country, and partly to a strong literary and cultural tradition of femininity, coquetry, and a desire to please men. In addition, close family ties stressing paternal domination and submission to discipline mitigated against women's liberation from male domination.[27]

'It has been said that "women make the morals", but it would be more correct to say that they *accept* them. Through a deplorable frivolity, by a wish to please at any price, they tacitly accept men's opinions and yield to their wishes.'[28] Another commentator sees the Frenchwoman's passive position more as a result of her satisfaction with her place in society than as a result of social oppression. 'The Frenchwoman in general was so satisfied with her position in the family, which often enabled her to manage her husband's business or at least share in the direction of his work, that she showed little interest in agitating for the vote.'[29]

Frenchwomen in the nineteenth century, then, lacked some political and legal power, but they were sufficiently contented with their influence not to feel the need to campaign openly for reform.

IV TAHITI

Tahitian women enjoyed more equality than their French counterparts. William Ellis, a nineteenth-century English missionary, who arrived in Polynesia in 1816 and left in 1822, described the life of the islanders as he experienced it during those six years with more objectivity than most contemporary observers. He noted that women engaged in domestic activities (cooking, making clothes, raising children) as opposed to 'labours of the plantation',[30] particularly when there had been European contact. Furthermore, 'at a time when European women were little more than chattels and slaves, women of Polynesia stood substantially on a social par with men. Sometimes sisters were socially superior to their brothers, wives superior to their husbands. The first born child, either male or female, always had highest rank within the family.'[31] A wife could transmit property claims through her mother's family rather than through her husband's, as long as no children were involved.[32] In addition, the presence of a queen as well as the right of succession through female lineage also accentuated the equality of women in this society.

Heterosexual relations were freer and more open in Polynesia than in France. All European commentators acknowledged that in Tahiti sexual activity was a natural way of life, permeating all daily functions.

From some of the opinions set down by the early European visitors to these Islands one could gain the impression that the inhabitants spent most of their time arranging, preparing for, and engaging in copulation. There was, of course, no Kinsey among the visitors . . . but from many kinds of evidence it is abundantly clear that the Maohis generally made use of opportunities for amours whenever they occurred.[33]

Just as sexual activity was more uninhibited in Tahiti, marriage arrangements were more easily formed there than in European societies, with either sex taking the initiative. In addition to more formal 'marriages', sexual encounters took place at earlier ages and in much freer circumstances than were common for the European missionaries who first recorded social life on the Polynesian Islands.

Nearly every source contains assertions about how early in life many Maohi girls began the practice – not just in the form of simulative play but of actual intercourse with virile males. Bligh, for example, stated that 'lower class' girls in particular began the practice at an early age, some starting '. . . even at the Age of 7 Years'.[34]

Women of the upper classes tended to be more faithful than those in the lower ones, but Maohi women in general were more generous with their sexual favours than the women Europeans were accustomed to meet. In addition, Polynesian women were also attracted to the merchandise (dry goods and hardware) which the Occidentals provided.

It is probably safe to say that most of the sexual encounters experienced by the European visitors had to be purchased at what came to be standard market prices, which, however, were subject to considerable fluctuation. . . . the commercial aspect [of sexual services] became more explicit when Europeans were involved.[35]

Since our record of Tahitian mores and culture is based on European reports, the anthropological and sociological studies are biased because they are filtered through a foreigner's perspective. The material written on Muslim, African, and Japanese societies will also reflect this 'Orientalist' attitude, as most of the studies I cite, like Loti's, were written by Western observers.

Although there were many differences between Maohi and French women, the desire to please men was notably similar in the two cultures.

> As it is one of the chief points of female education, in these happy isles, to learn the great art to please, they are instructed in all the means of gaining the affection of the males, of studying every winning art, and of habituating themselves to that sweetness of temper which never fails to merit the return of attachment, of friendship and love.[36]

V   AFRICA

'From birth an African woman is regarded as a simple humble creature who is to marry away from home . . . Her male counterpart is honored and respected as one to inherit the father's land.'[37] Unlike Tahitian women, African women had few rights and little personal freedom. Their lives were regulated by tribal customs and their marriages arranged – often when they were very young and sometimes even before birth. Marriage, as in most traditional societies, was and continues to be a financial transaction, and the bride was contractually linked to either an individual or the larger family unit. This means that if the initial intended were to die, he would be replaced by another member of the family. Similarly, if a misfortune were to occur to the fiancée, one of her sisters would be given in her stead. Any breach of contract could be settled in court.[38]

Life cycles were regulated by strong kinship ties, and marriages based on love were rare. Polygamy was popular, with tribesmen having anywhere from two to five wives while chieftains enjoyed up to 50 wives.[39] The acquisition of more wives was often for financial purposes – more women to till the soil or to provide more children.[40] Once a woman married her husband, she was

entitled to equal rights with all the other wives. The first wife and
the favourite wife enjoyed more power, however, then the others,
and they ruled the household. It is not surprising, therefore, that
jealousy occurred in this environment, and not infrequently,
women would poison their husbands because they acquired a
younger wife or preferred a different wife to the former favourite.[41]
No matter how many wives a man had, he was obligated to
provide them with 'everything necessary for their subsistence and
maintenance'.[42] Women committing adultery were severely
punished if the adultery was committed in the husband's house;
outside the home, they were given 'greater liberties'.[43] 'Adultery
is suppressed by custom, not because it is itself an infraction
against moral law, but because it constitutes, in the eyes of the
natives, an attempt at the ownership rights of the woman's
possessor (whether husband or fiancé).'[44]

Women in Africa, then, were regarded as property rather than
people, and their emotions and feelings were rarely, if ever,
considered in marriage transactions. As a result, they hardly ever
experienced those sentiments found in Western marriages based
on choice. Instead, these unions often found 'blind, jealous,
tyrannical passion, which ends by poisoning the rival or the
husband'.[45]

On the other hand, in some tribes, a woman who disliked her
husband could leave him, and move in with another man. In this
case, her first marriage would be considered annulled and the
second husband would become the legal father of her children.
Nor would this situation reflect adversely on the first husband.
However, the latter could reclaim his first wife at any time, as
well as her children. 'The traditional rights of . . . women – to
enter into contracts, and to easy divorce, for instance – exceed
those granted in most Western societies until very recently.'[46]

VI ISLAM

According to some commentators, the position of women in the
Middle East prior to Mohammed was quite good. Pre-Islamic
poetry indicated women 'enjoyed great prestige and were on
occasion celebrated for their bravery in battle'.[47] In addition, at
least one observer argues that polyandry and matrilineal

inheritance and descent dated back to ancient times.[48] By the seventh century, however, when Mohammed was born, Byzantine and Persian influences had undermined the favourable position of women, and women were frequently treated as little more than chattels and slaves. 'Thus, fathers could dispose of unwanted daughters through exposure at birth; they could marry daughters to husbands who might take additional wives and divorce all or any of the women they wished; and brothers could divide their inheritance without provision for their sisters.'[49]

Mohammed contributed much toward the amelioration of the position of women in Arabic society. Many Surahs in the Koran deal with women's rights and the manner in which men should treat their wives, daughters, and sisters. Although man is regarded as superior,[50] he is enjoined in numerous verses of the Koran to protect and care for women. All aspects of interpersonal relations are touched on in it: marriage, divorce, the care and feeding of children, the proper manner to clothe one's spouse, financial provisions for one's daughter and wife (wives), sexual conduct, manner of ablutions and prayer, etc. What is most remarkable is the concern for the feelings and sensibilities of women. The word 'kindness' appears frequently in the commands. Prior to Mohammed's legislation, men could divorce women at will; the new, more liberal legislation provided for divorce only for specifically stated reasons.[51]

Mohammed was a realist. Recognising that matrimony was essential for men, he put few restrictions on the choice of women for the believer. It was only essential that a potential wife be 'believing', not an adulteress, and not connected to the intended by certain specified relationships.[52] A man was permitted up to four wives, but only if he could treat them all equally. This last provision can almost be interpreted as supporting monogamy as few men can be so equitable to four spouses. Most commentators, however, agree that the Prophet's intention was to ensure that all wives receive fair treatment.[53]

As in African societies, one of the reasons for polygamy was certainly economic. A landowner needed more help in the fields and more hands to harvest, so several wives were preferable to one. In addition, polygamy meant more children who, in turn, would help their father. There were, undoubtedly, other reasons for polygamous practices. Polygyny was practised by the wealthy, as a means of displaying their affluence. The Sultan, of course, had his harem, but only four of the women in it were wives – the rest were concubines.

Divorce was sanctioned in the Koran for men but not for women.[54] A husband could divorce his wife at any time by speaking the appropriate words three times, and could not remarry her unless she had been married and divorced by a second husband. She, in turn, was unable to sue her husband for divorce except in the case of male impotence or 'child marriages before the age of puberty'.[55] Men were permitted to beat women, but they were also admonished to treat them with kindness and fairness.

In the Ottoman Empire, as in all Muslim countries, the male always reigned supreme. Society was highly stratified, with females dependent upon the males with whom they were associated. On the highest level were the female members of the Sultan's household. Below them were the women who comprised the households of the ruling élites: the powerful ulema, military officers, and administrative leaders. The less important members of these groups, together with the richer merchants, made up the next level. Lower down the scale were the women who were married to craftsmen and artisans. At the very bottom were those women who were unmarried, together with those who were affiliated with men who earned their livelihood by positions not socially esteemed (tanners, gravediggers, etc.)[56]

Each household, especially at the higher levels, was, in turn, highly stratified. The more important the household, the more significant were such distinctions. Whether one was a first wife or a fourth wife in the household of the Grand Vizier, for example, was a matter of great consequence for all concerned.

Regardless of their class, all Muslim women were veiled, a consequence of the restrictions placed on them as early as the sixteenth century. Initially, women were confined to the house and family, and later prevented from making public appearances, either in the marketplace or while travelling. The result of this seclusion was the veil, an isolating technique ensuring that women be kept apart from men; only when women worked in the fields were veils removed. Protection in public places soon led to guardianship at home, and the logical outcome of this policy was the harem.

Although the veil has traditionally been seen as a means for men to segregate women, the Surah in the Koran which forms the religious basis for the action states: 'Tell thy wives and thy daughters and the women of the believers to draw their cloaks close around them (when they go abroad). That will be better, that so they may be recognised and not annoyed.'[57]

Islam recognised potential female strength and intelligence by sanctioning education for women. However, the type of education advocated was different for the two sexes. In traditional Muslim society, learning for women consisted of memorisation of the Koran and a knowledge of Islamic precepts.[58] While this was also true for men, their training often exceeded these limited goals. By the Tanzimat era (1825–76), intellectuals sought emancipation for women and were intent on achieving literacy for them.

> They all agreed that Islam was not anti-feminist and that the pursuit of knowledge was an obligation for both men and women. Some even were in favour of giving women the opportunity to take up such male-dominated professions as medicine and pharmacy. In literature, women writers appeared and women's periodicals flourished.[59]

Despite these modern soundings and attempts at equality, women were still segregated from men, forced to wear the çarsaf (veil), and rarely educated beyond primary school. It was not until the Ataturk years (post-1919) that women began to share more widely in educational opportunities.

However, Muslim women fared better in terms of financial security than they did in educational opportunities. Mohammed was very concerned that women be cared for by men, and that they be provided for by their fathers in case they could not marry. As a result, Islamic property law was patterned after Roman law, where women were permitted property ownership. The liberal nature of the law was due to far-sighted ideas that the father might die or the husband might divorce the wife, so she needed to control her property permanently. 'Therefore, it has come about that during all the past centuries Mohammedan women have been free to buy or sell or alienate property, without control of any other person, and in fact without the signature of the woman herself no transfer of any kind could be made of her own property.'[60]

While it was theoretically possible for a woman to engage in commerce and trade, either with her spouse or as a sponsor or backer of someone else's business, in practice few did so. Most were content to engage in social rather than commercial or intellectual relationships, and were happy to live off the economy, rather than to contribute to it.[61]

All the changes which took place in the Ottoman Empire during the nineteenth century had a profound impact on the rôle of women in that society. Most importantly, Western ideas began to influence Ottoman women, some of whom became more politically aware and more socially active. Some even began to agitate for social reform.[62]

VII JAPAN

Despite the Occidental veneer over nineteenth-century Japanese society, traditional Eastern values dominated the culture. The influence of Buddhism and Confucianism preserved an enduring tradition of female inferiority and dependency. The long history of feudalism in the country led the Japanese to regard marriage as a political relationship. In the hierarchical society, each class approved of the marriages for the order below. Shoguns acted as matchmakers for feudal lords who, in turn, sanctioned the unions of their retainers and peasants. Through strict control, the system ensured loyalty and economic interdependence.[63] 'The subordination of the self to the needs of the collective family group was concordant with the more generalized notion of subordination of self to the national collectivity. *On* – unending obligation to parents – was the basis of loyalty to the father-Emperor.'[64]

Women, as in the other cultures studied, were little more than a commodity. Kaibara Ekken, a seventeenth-century moralist who wrote for the masses, expressed the general attitude toward women when he pronounced: ' "Such is the stupidity of her [the woman's] character that it is incumbent on her, in every particular, to distrust herself and obey her husband." '[65] Yet, despite their supposed lack of intelligence, women were expected to run the household. Except for this domestic responsibility, they were effectively excluded from participating in social life. They were discouraged from religious participation and encouraged to remain at home. As a result, they were isolated from other women. There was, of course, no contact with the opposite sex. In addition, they were prevented from receiving an education. 'It is well that women should be unlettered. To cultivate women's skills would be harmful. They have no need of learning.'[66]

A woman's place was as a wife and as a daughter-in-law. In this patrilocal society, she was expected to serve her parents-in-law first and then her husband. 'She must herself render to him the little services that a European expects of his valet. She must not only take care of his clothing, but must bring it to him and help him put it on, and must put away with care whatever he has taken off . . .'[67] Her first and foremost duty to her husband was obedience.

The importance of the family was so crucial, that all societal relations hinged upon it. The patriarchal family structure demanded strict obedience; all filial acts were committed to ensure the survival of the family and to perpetuate its good name. Children belonged to the entire family, not just to the parents. Thus 'the sale of a daughter in time of extreme need might save a house from ruin, and filial piety exacted submission to such sacrifice . . .'.[68] Not only was filial duty regulated, but sentiment and expression were subject to discipline as well. The Japanese were expected to suppress their emotions and even display contrary feelings. 'And in all classes demeanor was regulated so severely that even to-day the manners of the people everywhere still reveal the nature of the old discipline.'[69]

Succession was patrilineal, and in the event that the family produced only daughters, a son from another family was usually brought in to marry the eldest daughter. Ultimate authority in all matters lay with the family head. Although he was responsible for arranging good marriages within the family, and widows and divorcees were theoretically able to return to the family, in actuality a mismatch reflected badly upon him. As a result, divorce was frowned upon. Nevertheless, it was relatively easy for a man to obtain a divorce. He had only to write a short statement of his intention, 'known as "three lines and a half" indicating their brevity'[70] for a marriage to be dissolved. If a woman were widowed, the husband's family could 'send her away' – an effective 'divorce' measure. Should the woman wish to remarry after her husband's death, she required her in-laws' approval, and they rarely acquiesced to these demands.

Japanese women, then, were always at the mercy of men. Their lives were totally regulated and completely circumscribed by custom and culture, and their lack of education reinforced their inferior position. Even the music they were expected to play to entertain the male householders reflected their subordinacy.

The music of ancient Japan which women were privileged to learn was often quite difficult, but it was calculated to express passivity and resignation. Its minor key was to give vent to feelings that were sad and deep but which contained at the same time a spirit of resolution to make any required sacrifice.[71]

In this atmosphere, it was not surprising to find passive, dependent, submissive, and resigned females.

VIII   CONCLUSION

This brief analysis of the position of women in several disparate societies serves to indicate the nineteenth-century status and rights of women in those cultures. How did Loti describe them? Were the Oriental women he depicted in his novels modelled on a realistic product of any of these societies? Or were they cast in pre-conceived 'Occidental' moulds? According to our findings, Tahitian women were not subject to the same cultural constraints as Japanese or Turkish women. Does Loti's portrayal of a Rarahu, for example, resemble that of an Aziyadé? Or is the national condition of each heroine so different that the two female types could never be confused? To see how Loti manipulated his characters and to examine what characteristics all the Oriental women had in common, I will now turn to a critical review and appraisal of his fiction.

4

Loti and Women: a Re-evaluation

In the previous chapter, I examined the actual position of women in various nineteenth-century societies in order to determine whether the various Oriental women in Loti's novels conformed to reality or whether they were simply products of an over-worked, romantic, fictive vision. As the novels are discussed, the accuracy of the social reality described will become clear. But what about another reality, that of the woman as a thinking, feeling, individual personality? Does Loti try to understand her and provide motivation for her emotions and actions? Does he view her as a person or as a type? And what is her function for him? Is she an equal, a helpmate, a companion, or is she a servant, a sexual object, and an inferior being?

Traditionally, Loti has been regarded as an author who is sympathetic to women. Because he wrote books about women he knew, interacted with, and presumably loved, critics thought he presented both an accurate social description and a sensitive, compassionate portrayal of specific individuals. Basil Rafter, in discussing Suleima,[1] a young Moroccan prostitute whom Loti befriended and whose 'pure kiss' he cherished even though she was sentenced to death for poisoning three husbands, writes:

> This episode is an exact reproduction of that of the gypsy of Fontbruant. There is the same pity for a small, uncultivated being whose appearances hide, for Loti, a fundamental goodness, the same implicit respect for the woman and the same sentiment for the nobility of her true role.[2]

Another commentator affirms these positive feelings for women by stating: 'He is infinitely sensitive to feminine love.'[3]

Moreover, Loti was very popular with women, who must have felt that he spoke for their condition.

He was an irresistible figure in the 'nineties, not only to inexperienced, untravelled girls who might be expected to revel in arm-chair *déplacements* and tantalising mixtures of spirit and flesh ('Il était réservé à Pierre Loti de nous faire goûter jusqu'à l'ivresse, jusqu'à délire, jusqu'à la stupeur, l'âcre saveur des amours exotiques', wrote Anatole France, quite beside himself and voicing his contemporaries), but to *mondaine* hostesses in palmy salons, too.[4]

Still another observer reiterates this point of view when he states:

For women, this naval officer with his exotic adventures represented the lover-type, at the same time ardent and dreamer. They found themselves again in what he expressed [that was] tender and languorous, passionate and also pretty; they were grateful to him for idealising love without forgetting voluptuousness, and for making them the supreme reason for living.[5]

Despite these positive statements, Loti's treatment of Oriental women is troubling. For one thing, they are all invested with a certain sameness,[6] a lack of intellect, an attractive exterior concealing a generally simple but well-meaning disposition, and a desire to serve solely the handsome Occidental god who has somehow been miraculously transported to their native shores.

The young girls are all chaste and pure; the young women, on the other hand, are not, but they redeem their lack of chastity by a profound attachment to their lover. All are described exclusively according to masculine desire. They have no personal life and no value except in relation to that which binds them to the man they desire.[7]

Because Loti couches negative attitudes in positive terms, his mistreatment of women is insidious. Although he pretends to care for most of the Oriental women, and even to love them, he manages to focus on their faults. The females depicted are generally idle, self-indulgent, and vacuous.[8] They exist to please the men they attract (and never marry), and they become prostitutes or commit suicide when their lovers leave them.

In all the Oriental novels, an initial problem of communication exists between Loti and the women he favours. No matter how exotic the locale or how foreign in custom and language is the culture the sailor/hero visits, Loti overcomes the barrier in short order. He arrives in the new land, totally unable to speak its language, meets a young woman, and becomes intimate with her *before* he learns her tongue. On one level this indicates that love is a universal language requiring no semantic considerations, but on another level it points to a lack of interest in anything but sexual concerns. The woman is regarded as an object to be used for the author's benefit.

Then, in seemingly record time, Loti becomes fluent in each language, whether it be Japanese, Maori, or Turkish. Since all these tongues are very different linguistically, their mastery is no mean feat, and the reader is meant to be impressed with the author's abilities. Loti takes pains to indicate that he learns each one sufficiently well so that social intercourse is no longer problematic. This permits him to operate comfortably in a strange environment. In any event, his knowledge of grammar and vocabulary is always adequate for his needs *vis-à-vis* his mistress. Thus, Loti confronts languages in the same way he views women; he reduces and simplifies them to convenient uniformity. Their individuality is eradicated, and the vehicle of communication (whether linguistic or sexual) becomes another expression of masculine domination.

Interestingly, no matter how physically close he becomes with his paramour, he never shares his anxieties or fears with her. This is reserved for discourse with members of his Occidental family and friends. To these he confesses his insecurities, his doubts, and his fears of the 'néant'; to his Oriental mistress he presents himself as self-confident, culturally assimilated, and sexually potent. In truth, the daily life Loti describes in all his Oriental novels revolves around the love which all these simple women feel for him. Of all his partners, only Aziyadé inspires strong feelings on his part, and even these are inflated the further he is from the event. His alleged passion for her is posited wholly in sexual terms, although he insists on confusing it with love.[9]

In addition, all the Oriental women (with the exception of the Japanese who, according to Loti, are products of an artificial society) function mostly in a natural, out-of-doors environment. Seductions frequently take place in nature (for example, the gypsy in *Prime Jeunesse*, Aziyadé in the eponymous novel, Rarahu in *Le*

Mariage de Loti, Fatou-gaye in *Le Roman d'un spahi*). The open, primitive surroundings mirror the passionate inner emotions. Not only is the environment elemental, but all Loti's Oriental women are compared at various times with different animals – usually feline.

April-Shower and Matsuko, two *mousmés* featured in *Madame Chrysanthème* and *La Troisième Jeunesse du Mme Prune* are described as 'barbarians' and 'poor little marmosets'.[10] Tetuoara, a transplanted Melanesian in *Le Mariage de Loti*, is full of inexhaustible good humour and 'simian gaiety';[11] Rarahu and her best friend Tiahoui are seen as 'laughing little creatures who . . . frolicked like two flying fish'.[12] Japanese women 'look like little monkeys, like little china ornaments, like I don't know what',[13] and Djénane's servant, Kondja-Gul, is characterised as 'a dog faithful to excess'.[14] Cora, the French 'mulâtresse' in Senegal, Jean Peyral's unfaithful mistress, has a 'hideous expression of a beast which one has disturbed in its love-making',[15] while Fatou-gaye, Jean's saviour and future mistress, receives a thankful caress after she saves his life 'absolutely as though he set about scratching the neck of a large, wheedling tom-cat'.[16]

When the women are not being disparaged as small, defenceless creatures, the author treats them to uncomplimentary epithets.[17] Aziyadé, the little 'purchased slave girl', is compared with Faust's Marguerite, symbol of the fallen woman ('like Marguerite's soul, her soul was pure and virginal, even though her child's body, bought by an old man, was not so any more').[18] In *Prime Jeunesse*, the little industrious gypsy who sells home-made reed baskets for a living is dubbed 'little thieving gypsy'[19] even though there is no other mention of her thievery in the text. Rarahu's 'savage'[20] nature, prompted by coquettishness and greediness[21] permits her to accept gifts from an old, bony Chinaman, the veritable incarnation of corruption. Finally, loyal Fatou, who saved Jean Peyral's life after his unhappy love affair with Cora, is subjected to inhuman vilification for selling his watch ('Here was this Fatou who, for the last four years had taken from him his money, his dignity, his life!').[22] 'The propensity to debase the love object' is intimately related to Loti's need for sexual relations with women of a lower class than the one to which he belonged, or women who were intellectually inferior to him.

If a man does not desire any woman who is his equal or even his superior – may it not be that he is protecting his threatened self-regard in accordance with that most beautiful principle of sour grapes? From the prostitute or the woman of easy virtue one need fear no rejection, and no demands in the sexual, ethical, or intellectual sphere. One can feel oneself superior.[23]

These Oriental heroines, then, suffer from verbal abuse and unflattering comparisons. In addition, they are not even dignified with unique character traits; Loti portrays them stereotypically. The gypsy wears a red silk scarf at her throat and sports large gold earrings, Aziyadé peers through the grille windows of her harem home, Rarahu walks half-naked in her *pareo*, and Fatou-gaye clings obsessively to her soldier-lover. The women lack individuality and personality, and seem to exist only for the hero's delectation. In point of fact, there is no conflict between Loti and any of the women he depicts; he finds a female, decides he wants her, and she immediately submits to his advances. His charms are so apparent that his goal is always readily attainable. In this male fantasy world, all desirable women are for the asking, and they never form a real centre of interest for the reader (except, perhaps, in the case of Djénane in *Les Désenchantées*) because they are so flat and one-dimensional. As Barthes aptly states about *Aziyadé* (although it is equally applicable to most of the 'Oriental' novels), nothing happens and the discourse in the novel points to emptiness; 'doesn't he tell us [of] the emptiness of the discourse through which human relationships constitute themselves?'.[24]

The real reason for Loti's lack of interest in human relationships is that he is basically concerned with only one person – himself.[25] His narcissism causes him to portray himself as hero in most of the Oriental works, and his prowess at overcoming all barriers, linguistic, cultural, and sexual, serves as wish-fulfilment. Although nominally the centre of each novel is a different Oriental woman, in actuality the real protagonist is Loti. Thus, Loti uses Oriental women as a means of self-aggrandisement. Through their presence he indicates to the reader that he is linguistically adept, socially and culturally flexible, sexually vigorous, physically appealing (all the heroines are very attractive and they fall in love with him instantly), and always completely in command.

In three of the novels (*Mariage*, *Aziyadé*, and *Fantôme*) he actually uses his pseudonym for the name of the hero. In the other works, the protagonist is clearly Loti's *alter ego*, and the author follows a time-honoured tradition which conceives of a character as little more than a vehicle for the exploration of the author's personality.

> In imitation of Chateaubriand, certain of our writers – Loti and Barrès particularly, see in the literary application that foreign themes afford them, only a means of enriching their sensibility and analyzing their 'self-hood': Japan or Spain, Senegal, Tahiti or Venice certainly offer them splendid countrysides and curious mores to study. *Their essential goal remains no less than the observation of their own personality*. [Author's italics.][26]

Sometimes he appears with another name (André Lhéry in *Les Désenchantées*, Jean Peyral in *Le Roman d'un spahi*), sometimes his characters mouth his sentiments without identifying themselves as Loti (*Fleurs d'ennui*), and sometimes the novels are clearly autobiographical, where the chief character is a nameless 'I' (*Madame Chrysanthème*, and *La Troisième Jeunesse de Mme Prune*). In the famous Preface to *Madame Chrysanthème*, the author clearly states that the title of the book is misleading, as he, and not Madame Chrysanthème, is the chief character of the work:

> This is the journal of a summer of my life, in which I have changed nothing, not even the dates . . . Although the longest rôle appears to be that of Madame Chrysanthème, in reality the three principal characters are *Me*, *Japan*, and the *Effect* the country has produced on me.[27]

Roland Barthes perceives the ambiguity of the situation Loti creates for himself through the *dédoublement* of Loti as both character and author in *Aziyadé*.

> Loti is the hero of the novel (even if he has other names and even if this novel poses as the account of a reality not of a fiction): Loti is *in* the novel (the fictive creature, Aziyadé, calls her lover ceaselessly *Loti*: 'Look, Loti, and tell me . . .'); but he is also outside, since the Loti who has written the book doesn't coincide at all with the hero Loti: they haven't the same identity: the first Loti is English, he dies young; the second Loti, first-named Pierre, is a member of the Académie française, he has written many other books than the account of his Turkish loves.[28]

The confusion in identities is further complicated by the fact that Pierre Loti itself is a pseudonym for Louis Marie Julien Viaud, and Barthes indicates that what is unusual here is that the real Viaud coined his pen name from his protagonist. In addition, the fictional Loti adopts the Turkish name 'Arif', in order to further disguise himself as a native while he lives in Eyub with Aziyadé. Thus the question posed is *who is* Loti, and where do we find him?

In fact, it is Loti's quest for himself and his identity that constitutes the motive force of his oeuvre and he uses the Oriental woman as a screen for finding and defining himself. The easy seductions, the worshipful attitudes of the women serve to enhance a weak sense of male identity. Through her he can exorcise a negative self-image by displacing his own sense of inferiority on to her person. This accounts for his need to inject some negative epithet or some unflattering statement about the heroine, even when there is no apparent cause for the critical comment. In several of the texts he will note that the women appear as though they have no intellect ('What thoughts are running through that little brain? . . . Moreover, it is a hundred to one that she has no thoughts whatever'),[29] no morality ('No one had taught her [Aziyadé] any moral principles which could put her on guard against herself'),[30] and as though they are culturally and intellectually inferior ('She [Rarahu] understood vaguely that there must have been gulfs, in the intellectual domain, between Loti and herself, entire unknown worlds of ideas and knowledge').[31] Clearly Loti needs to debase women in order to assert his masculine superiority: 'When we cannot understand something, we always fall back on abuse. An excellent way of making a task lighter.'[32]

The repeated instances of verbal deprecation point to both fear of and suppressed hatred toward women. In the case of

unconscious hatred . . . sadistic components of love have, from constitutional causes, been exceptionally strongly developed, and have consequently undergone a premature and all too thorough suppression . . . the neurotic phenomena . . . arise on the one hand from conscious feelings of affection which have become exaggerated as a reaction, and on the other hand from sadism persisting in the unconscious in the form of hatred.[33]

Homosexuals (and we know that Loti was at least bisexual if not homosexual) frequently need to vilify women as a compensatory mechanism to deal with their guilt for their own sexual persuasions.

Since no human being can easily face his own compulsions, the male tends to project his fears and antagonisms in terms of derogatory attributes by insisting that women are evil, inferior and valueless (because different) and hence should be made to obey, be kept in their place, or fulfill some unreal role which neutralizes them and removes them from the sphere of competition.[34]

Loti's Oriental women are frequently victims of physical or mental abuse (Aziyadé, Djénane, Fatou-gaye, and Rarahu) and the author delights in asserting his (or his *alter ego*'s) superiority over the hapless female. They are clearly products of a phallocentric imagination which needs attractive, loving, hero-worshipping characters to enhance a weak male image. Although Loti, the protagonist, appears happy to receive their attention, he is also contemptuous of them. Clearly these attitudes are merely transpositions of Loti's, the author's, own sentiments.[35]

To what can we attribute this? It appears that Loti's anxiety toward women manifested itself in a castration complex,[36] and that he compensated for these fears by castigating his submissive heroines. One critic speaks to male fears of the opposite sex when he states that there is 'a wealth of evidence which demonstrates that the male attitude toward female sexual functions is basically apprehensive; women, in short, are dangerous'.[37] This fear is universal; one finds the same myths recurring in different cultures and different traditions world-wide, and their similarity can only account for the presence of deep-seated fears of women among men. Specifically, this masculine fear is located in the unconscious and subconscious fear of the vagina and its castrating effects. Jean-Paul Sartre expresses it as '"Beyond any doubt her (the woman's) sex is a mouth and a voracious mouth which devours the penis – a fact which can easily lead to the idea of castration. The amorous act is the castration of the man."'[38]

On a more mythic level, Hays recounts a North American Indian folk tale dealing with a folk hero who was enticed by a bad witch to marry her daughters. Her companion, a good witch, warned him secretly that the two daughters were dangerous, as their vaginas contained teeth which would bite off his penis (this phenomenon is known as 'vagina dentata'). The remainder of the tale narrates the hero's adventures as he sets out to marry one of the daughters after nullifying her lethal power. In the course of his escapades he finds two whetstones; he thrusts one up the first daughter's sex organ as far as it would go, thus killing her (note the violence of the act) and then he takes the second whetstone, files the teeth down in the sister's vagina while she is sleeping, and ultimately runs off with his now-harmless bride.[39]

Karen Horney explained that male fear of females appeared in the dreams of all her male analysands and that

> 'the dread of the female genital is extended to dread of women in general.' Everywhere the man strives to rid himself of his dread of women by objectifying it. 'It is not,' he says, 'that I dread her; it is that she herself is malignant, capable of any crime, a beast of prey, a vampire, a witch, insatiable in her desires. She is the very personification of what is sinister.'[40]

These feelings are particularly strong during adolescence when the immature boy is unsure how he should behave toward the opposite sex and is apprehensive as to what the female will do to him. In extremely neurotic cases, dread of the vagina is never overcome, and homosexuality results.[41] Loti certainly fits this pattern. Ultimately, 'just as coitus is in a certain sense . . . castration death appears as the final coitus or castration of life.'[42] Loti's early books in particular end with the heroine's death, and *Fantôme d'orient* chronicles a search for Aziyadé conducted under a shadow of death. This unhappy experience will be replicated in *Les Désenchantées*, in which the heroine, Djénane, exerts her strong attraction for Loti primarily because she reminds him of Aziyadé. Here, too, the heroine commits suicide, a final, wilful castration of life.

Another interpretation for the frequent deaths of his fictional heroines is that Loti had a morbid need to be loved and to suffer as a result of that love. Moreover, this feeling was almost pathological, and so intense that he needed to convert any feeling of love into suffering.

> We believe that a fatal desire to make himself loved and then to suffer from this exists in him. We will see later that in terms of

the women he loved, he often suffered morally. This appetite for suffering seems to us to frequently approach a neuropathic state. Here is a matter of pure masochism.[43]

Not only does masochism explain Loti's relations with women, but it also accounts for his constant dissatisfaction with life, his need to leave any given spot in order to search for another, preferably more primitive, area, and his restlessness once he arrives at the longed-for destination. Millward attributes Loti's feeling of 'ennui', his need for escape, to 'this masochism which manifests itself again in this complex of dissatisfaction, of discontent, in this impossibility of permitting himself the least happiness without which something might come to trouble him'.[44]

All Loti's experiences with Oriental heroines take place on foreign soil except one – his first. Here the gypsy represents the exotic, the 'other', and the episode in *Prime Jeunesse* will prove paradigmatic for all the author's future attachments.[45] Not only is the erotic incident a model for future love affairs, but all the themes which have just been detailed and which will appear in Loti's 'Oriental' novels emerge in this short, twenty-page event. Since this autobiography is one of the author's last works (published in 1919, four years before his death), it may be that by that time, the various threads with which he customarily wove the tapestry of his fiction were so familiar and often-used that he was able to combine them when recounting this vignette. Whatever the reason, the gypsy episode provides Loti with a perfect synthesis of all his ideas, and provides an ideal entrée into the textual discussion of how Loti manipulated women in his literary oeuvre.

Prime Jeunesse deals with Loti's thirteenth to seventeenth years, and in it he describes his 'initiation into manhood' with the little, nameless gypsy girl. The young sixteen-year old Julien has left his home to go on vacation for the first time by himself, a visit to his married sister in Fontbruant. His anticipation of adventure is keen, but it is accompanied by an 'unquenchable need [which] caused me genuine suffering'.[46] He arrives at his destination, and that evening, as he goes out on the terrace to visit some friends of his brother-in-law, he overhears them speaking of 'a certain handsome gypsy, wild and unapproachable',[47] who was camped with her clan by the forest entrance. He is immediately attracted to her, and although they exchange no words, she turns back to look at him as she leaves, which unnerves him and causes him to indicate 'that her last look, for me alone, was softened by a faint smile'.[48] Here we find the conjunction of several recurring themes: the initial contact made out-of-doors, the non-verbal intercourse, the instant mutual attraction, the need for suffering, and most particularly, the exotic nature of the temptress, who is a member of a non-Occidental group.

Lack of verbal communication marks their first meeting; instead of speech, glances and body language serve to attract the young Julien to his first mistress. Since the gypsy speaks French poorly ('a vague French mixed with Spanish')[49] they hardly speak during their entire week-long relationship; as a matter of fact, their first kiss is exchanged before the youngster ever hears his girlfriend's voice.[50]

Linguistic differences are not the only mark of the 'exotic' for Loti; he also associates foreignness with bestiality. He finds the gypsy to be wild, animal-like, sunburned, and reminiscent of both Eritrea and India. Her eyes 'hid all the sensual mysticism of India' while her colouring was that of 'the old baked earths of Eritrea'.[51] These comparisons with far-off exotic lands, couched in clichés, characterise the female. The natural imagery continues in Loti's description of the young temptress, who came close to the sixteen-year old virgin 'with the little indirect manner of a cat who is afraid of scaring away her prey'.[52] She is spoken of as 'a wolf' and 'a creature' (p. 135). Moreover, Loti makes a point of indicating that this first sexual experience is associated forever in Julien's memory with the fine swarm of dragonflies which flew around them in their outdoor ravine. By extension, then, Julien links the gypsy with insects as well.

Here, as in so many of his other 'Oriental' works, Loti heightens his emphasis on nature by having the sexual experience take place outdoors. Fornication occurs in a ravine full of underbrush, tangled vegetation, large ferns, and wild plants. Curiously, the initiation into manhood takes place 'before one of these grotto entrances which resemble the porticoes of a Cyclopean temple'.[53] More explicit 'vagina dentata' imagery could hardly be forthcoming. The natural, wild setting stands in sharp contrast to the innocent 'chambrette blanche' at his sister's house, Julien's vacation home. Later sexual escapades will find the sailor/writer seducing his new love in a rowboat on the Bosphorus (*Aziyadé*), sleeping on the grass entwined in his girlfriend's arms (*Le Mariage de Loti*), and describing his hero's 'nuptial couch' in *Le Roman d'un spahi* in front of a huge baobab tree on the Sorr marsh. In each case, sexuality is heightened by the vivid presence of nature.

The visually suggestive account of Julien's first seduction is reinforced by the narration of a dream which he had the evening before the actual event. Clearly his unconscious presages reality, for his dream almost exactly duplicates the events of the following day. He describes a beautiful, warm, romantic night which bewitched him[54] and his thoughts reverted to the gypsy who, he speculated, was probably sleeping at that moment, 'between the tawny arms of someone of her tribe'.[55] Here again, the imputation of sexual license is interesting, because his previous description of her had been that she was 'wild and unapproachable' ('farouche et inabordable'). He dreamed that he was 'in the middle of dense woods, in obscurity, clearing with great effort a passage among the underbrush and weeds'[56] when he became aware of other people around him who were the gypsies, including, of course, his intended.

Despite his attraction her, he distances himself from her by refusing to dignify her with a name; throughout the episode (both in the dream and its real-life counterpart) she is called 'la Gitane' or 'la belle Gitane', and frequently she is mentioned only as 'elle'. Her namelessness is symptomatic of her lack of individuality – she is *a* gypsy, but she could be any gypsy. She is portrayed stereotypically, both in her dress (complete with red silk neckerchief, flashy jewellery, and large golden earrings) and her physical features (thick, dark hair, statuesque appearance, long-necked and open-throated to display more body than a non-bohemian), so that she appears as little more than a pastiche of commonplaces.

Even the sexual experience resonates familiar conventions: the two figures manage to grope toward one another and then 'the beautiful gypsy, struggling at my sides against the creepers which more and more entwined our feet'[57] finally fell with him in the tangled rushes, and there he experienced his first sexual encounter. The density of the underbrush and the entwining vines form a thick, almost suffocating environment for coitus; the words 'petite mort', used to describe his dreamed orgasm, connote an ecstasy beyond life itself.

One does not need to be a psychoanalyst to see the explicit sexual imagery associated with the dense underbrush and tangled vegetation. Loti's sexual fears, prefigured in the dream and corroborated by fictional reality, are all too evident here. The dense underbrush with entwining vines has all the earmarks of castration anxiety. On the other hand, the strong, maternal influence which guided him throughout his life is also evident in the grotto imagery. The desire to find, particularly in the actual seduction scene, 'some still more inviolable nook, in this ravine whose shadowy entanglement was already a sufficient hiding place'[58] recalls a return to the womb, a desire to bury himself within the nurturing body from whence he came. Nature, the Earth-mother, becomes a surrogate for the real mother from whom he is parted on this first trip alone away from Rochefort. Just prior to this episode, he indicated in his autobiography that 'for the first time in the sixteen years that I existed, I felt cruelly the very clear feeling of proceeding *alone* in an ephemeral life'.[59] The fear of loneliness, the need to ward off what he would later term 'le néant', will sound another recurrent theme in the Loti oeuvre.

Like her other Oriental sisters, the nameless gypsy seducing (or being seduced by) the Occidental is simpler, more naïve, and more unsophisticated than her lover, even if she is more sexually mature. As is so often the case in this author's canon, the superior Westerner imagines that his refinements attract the primitive native, even when she does not articulate this need. *Prime Jeunesse* gives us a perfect example of Loti's projections stated as truths. Since he exchanged few words with the seductive gypsy, he could only conjecture about what attracted her to him. 'Undoubtedly she had guessed my refinements, which astonished and charmed her savage nature.'[60] Since he was attracted to her animal-like wildness, he assumed that she would be equally captivated with someone radically opposite to herself. However, their lack of communication prevented him from knowing and understanding her feelings, so we cannot rely on his anlysis for an understanding of what attracted her to him. This trait (treating suppositions as though they were certainties) would become a characteristic of Loti's writing.

Moreover, the inferences that the author draws about Oriental women, even when he presumes to love them, are frequently condescending and negative. His attitude toward the little gypsy girl is symptomatic of this; when he describes her beautiful eyes he states: 'what fascinated above all, was her eyes of depth and of

night, – behind which, who knows, *there was perhaps nothing
. . . .*.[61] Loti's assumption of the gypsy's stupidity is more revealing
of the author than of the character he is portraying. Nothing he
has written about her heretofore has in any way prepared the
reader to find her stupid. Until this editorial comment she is
depicted as industrious, ambitious, and enterprising as she sells
the baskets she made herself to as many natives and tourists as
she could find. Since their language barrier prevented effective
communication, Julien had never conversed with her; why then
would he assume ignorance and stupidity on her part? He might,
like most of his contemporaries, have assumed that all gypsies are
mentally inferior, men as well as women. On the other hand, he
might either have felt threatened by her or it is possible that he
needed to feel superior at her expense. Perhaps her physical
domination of him, her self-confidence and lack of fear in sexual
matters inspired him to retaliate by asserting his perceived mental
superiority. Here Loti's memoirs proclaim both cultural and
masculine supremacy.

In addition to inferences of mental inferiority, Loti refers to the
gypsy with his usual gratuitous and uncomplimentary adjectives.
She is described as a 'little thieving gypsy', 'daughter of a race of
pariahs', and 'the lowest of the low', and her sunburned hand is
'as expert at committing thefts in the farms as it is at plaiting
reeds into baskets'.[62] The negative adjectives and unflattering
epithets, although conforming to the usual gypsy stereotypes,
seem gratuitous here, since the reader is never acquainted with a
single instance of her wrongdoing. Based on Loti's description of
the gypsy's métier, we can only assume that she was a hard-
working young teenager who made baskets to help support
her tribe. The subversion must then point either to Loti's
preconceptions about gypsies or to the purposeful omission of
negative information. In any event, the characterisation of the no-
named Bohemian makes us realise that Loti harbours negative
views about women.

One more characteristic of Loti's treatment of Oriental women
must be noted: the general pattern in the 'Oriental' novels is for
Loti or his protagonist to leave the indigene and for her either to
commit suicide or to die. Because the emotional investment in the
gypsy is so slight (as it is in the two books on Japan, *Madame
Chrysanthème* and *Mme Prune*) the mistress is permitted to remain
alive after leaving, or being left by, the male. As soon as a hint of

reciprocal friendship or sexual involvement occurs, the hero is portrayed as being in complete command. Thus, it is he who determines the outcome of the relationship. Loti's phallocentric imagination continually structures situations and associations so that the masculine perspective emerges victorious.

5

Loti the Exploiter

Loti was very much a product of the nineteenth century. He was not an original thinker, and he readily accepted current conventional values. As we have already noted, he subscribed to the notion that women were, by definition, inferior to men. Their function was to serve their masters, making life as comfortable for them as possible. In return, the male would provide food and shelter, and introduce his female companion (or bride) to life's wider horizons – with which he was familiar, but of which she was necessarily ignorant.

Women were classified, categorised, and simplified by this mentality. Their individuality was stripped away from them as they were summarily forced into preconceived aesthetic and sexual moulds. The simple, pure virgin was juxtaposed against the sensual temptress;[1] the persecuted maiden acted as a foil against 'La Belle Dame Sans Merci' – the cruel vampire woman who was ready to suck the life marrow from her innocent male partner's body.[2] Nineteenth-century attitudes towards the woman find her 'variously anaesthetic, a martyr to her husband's sexuality, mysterious, dangerous, a castrator, a source of soft contamination and someone who forced reluctant men to grow up'.[3]

These attributes certainly applied to the Occidental female; images of the Oriental woman, on the other hand, were inevitably accompanied by those of indolence, sexual expertise, and voluptuous degradation. Her presumed highly developed eroticism and innate sensuality formed the Western paradigm for the 'dark lady', the 'black Venus', and the Fatal Woman. This stereotyping reflected prevalent feelings of Western superiority, both toward the Easterner and toward the woman.

Loti endorsed these Romantic viewpoints and imbued his heroines with contemporary normative attitudes. Like his countrymen, he attributed intelligence and wisdom in Oriental women only to old age,[4] preferring to find young Oriental women flighty, ignorant, loving, and totally devoted to their Occidental lovers, whom they worshipped for their handsome bodies as well as their superior minds. By articulating and promulgating prevailing attitudes, Loti ratified popular opinion. Moreover, the pattern of 'loving, leaving and grieving'[5] which he established early in his work satisfied his vanity – by creating fictional characters who were dependent upon and very much in love with him or his male protagonist, Loti inflated his own importance and that of his fictional *alter ego*; by mourning the deaths of the women, he elevated their stature only to indicate that they were worthy of his and his heroes' grief.

Loti exploited women by using them to further his own aims. By and large he established heterosexual relationships less for the particular companionship than for the fulfilment of egocentric desires. Men provided him with the friendship and the intellectual support he craved; women provided the vehicle for self-aggrandisement. Oriental women represented a means by which the French author could attain several goals – through them he could acquire a deeper and more authentic knowledge of the country visited than he could as a tourist, through them he would have his physical needs met, through them he could ward off loneliness, and best of all, he could hide behind their screen when engaging in debauchery. Finally, women provided him with an opportunity for self-comprehension; as he examined his relationships with them, he explored his own feelings and reactions (always the subject of keenest interest to him), and his fictional creations as well as his diary entries, furnished the record of his introspection.

Loti constantly battled against a personal emptiness, a feeling of 'ennui' derived from the general *fin de siècle* atmosphere in France, coupled with his own unsuccessful search for religion. 'He was afflicted with a feeling of the worthlessness of life, with the ennui of his own existence, and with a profound fear of death, without hope of immortality.'[6] This was due to his background (see Chapter 2) for, as Lerner has noted:

Loti's problem was not easily curable; the traditional stability of faith, hearth, and family was no longer able to support him after the disillusioning effects of the death of his brother and his childhood sweetheart, and the family's bankruptcy; the desires and deceptions of the outside world had severed his spiritual and moral links with the past; the real world of the senses, of nature and evolution, the frailty of the human condition and inevitable coming of death had shattered them.[7]

Over and over again in his writing, Loti attempts to fend off the inevitable, to counteract the impending vision of nothingness and death, and women serve as one distraction from this fear. Loti regards them less in terms of lasting emotional attachments than as useful instruments with which to protect himself against loneliness, 'le néant', and ennui. Through their companionship and presence, they provide a distraction from the 'disgusting emptiness and the immense ennui of living'.[8] Loti's candour led him to admit to one of his reasons for forming relationships; in the case of Madame Chrysanthème, he writes:

Because of *ennui*, my God, because of loneliness, I had come, little by little, to imagine and to desire this marriage. And then, above all, to live a while *on solid ground*, in a shadowy nook amidst trees and flowers, how tempting that was, after these long months which we had just spent in the Pescadores (which are warm and sinister islands, without greenery, without woods, without streams, exuding the odour of China and of death). [Author's italics][9]

Loti's first few feverish encounters with Aziyadé in the small boat on the sea, when the author is overwhelmed with sexual passion and lust, are summarised in the sentence: 'I accept, in closing my eyes, everything which can make up for one hour the frightful emptiness of life, everything which is a semblance of friendship or of love.'[10] In addition, Aziyadé helps Loti to endure his stay in Salonika.[11]

Like Loti, the protagonist in *Aziyadé*, Jean Peyral, the hero of *Le Roman d'un spahi*, is also a victim of ennui. 'Ennui had come quickly to find poor Jean. It was a kind of melancholy which he had never felt, vague, indifinable, which began with nostalgia for his mountains, nostalgia for his village and for the thatched cottage of his beloved old parents.'[12] The African heat, the monotonous existence, the dead city, the far-off sounds of battle against the Boubakar-Ségou forces – all conspire to create a feeling of inescapable indolence in the young spahi. One way Jean finds of staving off the hopeless boredom of these unchanging surroundings is his affair with Fatou-gaye, 'a little black soul', a 'dissembler, liar . . . with an unbelievable admixture of malice and perversity'.[13]

But three years after his arrival, long after his liaison with Fatou-gaye had begun, 'Jean passed through different moral phases: he experienced highs and lows; most often he felt only a vague ennui, a lassitude before all things; and then, from time to time, home-sickness, which seemed dormant in his heart, overwhelmed him again to make him suffer.'[14] Peyral's weakness is his inertia – his inability to leave Africa for his home and his long-suffering, faithful mother and fiancée. The Occidental women are depicted as loyal and uncomprehending of their son/fiancé's new life; they become unwitting victims of the African heat and the strange, exotic mentality which seduces their son/lover away from them.

Just as Peyral relieves the tedium of his existence in Africa with a little native, so Loti, the sailor, diverts himself with local female inhabitants in *La Troisième Jeunesse de Mme Prune*. Here the author states: 'I was bored, and the idea came to me to distract myself, to have recourse to geishas.'[15] In this work, women serve not only as distractions from the tedium of life, but also as helpmates to combat the fear of isolation. 'No matter where fate had exiled you, a young and feminine soul (whose somewhat charming appearance is still a necessary enticement) [must] come to help you [ward off] the great loneliness.'[16]

Not only is the French writer bored, but his characters, too, reflect the world-weariness he feels. Ennui haunts the volume *Fleurs d'ennui*. In the short story, 'Les Trois Dames de la Kasbah', Loti describes six sailors on leave in Algiers, who get drunk and 'circulate' throughout the city for lack of anything better to do. They roll from one cabaret to another, stop briefly in a brothel, throw away their money recklessly, and finally meet three women who beckon them to enter their high-walled establishment. The sailors are drunk from boredom: 'They weren't afraid, they were only bored.'[17] Furthermore, 'these three ladies were very bored, because as long as the day lasted, they had nothing to do'. 'The whole day these three ladies were bored in their old, white prison.' 'They were as though plunged into an immense sadness, in a drunken stupor, daughters of a condemned race, enduring fatal things with a mournful resignation.'[18]

The women entice the three Basque sailors into their home, and the Occidentals enjoy an evening of pleasure with their Oriental whores. But morning comes, and with it, awareness of the women with whom they had been sleeping. Barazère, one of the sailors, looks at his partner. 'He saw that she was old, that her face was wrinkled and her flesh sagged. He turned away in horror, pushing her away with his foot.'[19] The women here serve the purpose of relieving the sailors' boredom, but the men are depicted as innocents led astray in an Oriental maze. They are lured by a painted, bejewelled ('as an idol') lady to leave their Breton cohorts and enter the 'little sinister door'. As 'priestesses' in an idolatrous temple they 'kept between themselves the secret and the blemish of a crime'.[20] Their crime is to be syphilitic, and to transmit their disease 'almost unconsciously' to the Europeans. Barazère, the young sailor who slept with the old mother, dies of the illness, whereas his companions spread the 'germes de mort' to their brides. It is their first-born sons who will suffer most, as they are covered with 'shameful-looking' sores at birth.

In this story, then, the penalty for trying to avoid an evening of boredom is generationally-inflicted punishment. The close-knit, chaste village in which the Bretons live will henceforth be infected by the Oriental malady. It is the Oriental woman who provides the momentary diversion from ennui, but her legacy is far-reaching and profoundly destructive.

This tale is interesting from several points of view. The usual pattern wherein European imperialism destroys Oriental societies is reversed here as Loti depicts the foreign civilisation as adversely affecting his own. Furthermore, the reader's sensibilities are manipulated to empathise with the European sailors. Not only is the blame for syphilis laid squarely in the laps of the Oriental women (who must, after all, have acquired the illness from men), but the Occidental responds to the plight of the sailors rather than that of their Basque and Breton brides who give birth to infected children. The 'healthy, vigorous' peasant stock is now tainted, but Loti does not dwell on the wives' predicament; instead, he singles out the first-born *sons* as requiring our sympathy. The moral of the tale, that 'it is always wrong to try to harm people, particularly when they are good, affectionate dears like those in this story'[21] incriminates those who inflict harm on the blameless – once again, the Oriental woman.

In 'Suleima', another tale in this collection, Loti, the character, fends off the ennui of his stay in Algeria by forming a relationship with a young prostitute whom he had known ten years earlier when she was still a child. Here he rationalises his debauchery by hiding behind his ever-present conceit. Suleima, the young girl who sells her body, accepts his money the morning after, but Loti flatters himself that her farewell kiss to him was not purchased. 'Besides, no gold piece could pay back a spontaneous kiss given by a charming young girl of sixteen.'[22] Loti cannot acknowledge that any woman – even one who dispenses 'love' professionally – would be immune to his considerable personal charm.

Oriental women, then, provide companionship *against* fear – fear of death, of boredom, and of unhappiness. At the same time, they play a positive rôle, for they serve to indoctrinate him into the indigenous culture. Both Aziyadé[23] and Djénane spend much of their time with the author explaining Turkish customs and the Moslem religion to him.[24] Djénane, Mélek, and Zeyneb, the heroines of *Les Désenchantées*, try to make Loti understand the plight of the Turkish woman, accentuating their Occidental education within an Oriental society and the religious conflict which this engenders, leading to their cultural displacement ('Here is the secret of the Moslem soul, in Turkey, in year 1322 of the Hegira. Our present education has led us to this split in our being.').[25]

Although Loti appreciates the social and cultural insights he gleans from his Turkish friends, nothing replaces first-hand experience for him. By moving in with an indigene, the Occidental voyager is better able to understand the exotic locale – and this is one of Loti's prime motives for domestication. By befriending or 'marrying' an indigene, Loti becomes involved in the life of his new acquaintance, and through her, the community in which she lives. Thus he counters his feelings of emptiness while acquiring new insights into the adoptive country. Another reason the French author moves in with a native is to be accepted by the society; Queen Pomaré's argument for 'marriage' with Rarahu is most persuasive: 'Loti, why not marry little Rarahu from the Apiré district? That would be much better, I assure you, and it would give you added standing in the country.'[26]

Although all the heroes in the 'Oriental' oeuvre are presented as attracted to women, not all of them are immediately anxious to yoke themselves to an indigene. Sometimes lassitude or circumstances conspire to link the Occidental hero to his Oriental paramour. The strange relationship between Jean Peyral and

Fatou-gaye is described negatively rather than positively; as a matter of fact, Loti takes pains not to explain the reasons for their mutual attraction, as though inter-racial fascination were incomprehensible. When he does speak of their relationship, he uses words like 'horreur', 'bizarre', 'impure', and 'atonie morale', and portrys the Negress in unflattering terms as having 'something *not human* [about her] which was terrifying'. She, like her Tahitian and Turkish sisters, is 'chosifiée'.[27]

> The spahi made of his black mistress his thing, an object which adorns his home, an animal which obeys him and on whom he imposes his will, but an animal who drives him to despair because between them, there exists the gulf of the races. He knows that he will never be able to feel pleasure like this being of another sex and another race [does]. As to sexual relations, Loti does not scorn women of other races, but he always remains the refined white man. He has transmitted his prejudices to his characters. The spahi considers the black woman like 'a fruit swollen with toxic juices full of unhealthy sensual pleasures', a veritable living snare.[28]

The 'snare' Fatou lays for him is her strange, exotic attraction, described in negative rather than positive terms. 'He was powerless to separate himself from her'[29] is the explanation that the narrator gives for the liaison between the white soldier and his black mistress.

Nor is this the only example of union between an Occidental and an Oriental based on reasons other than affection. In *Le Mariage de Loti*, forces outside the hero operate to bring Loti together with Rarahu. Here Rarahu's parents and the Queen provide the excuse for Loti's 'marriage' with the young Tahitian.[30] As though to confirm the impossibility of true love between an Occidental man and an Oriental woman, Plumkett, Loti's wise counsellor and *alter ego* in *Aziyadé*, intuits that his friend's grand passion is not all it appears to be: 'Be very careful not to confuse what is in her with what is in you. All our illusions stem from that: attributing what is in ourselves and nowhere outside of ourselves to what pleases us.'[31] Rarely, in any of these situations, is the word 'love' enunciated as the reason for the attachment. Fallah-Najmeh correctly points out that Aziyadé as individual was less important to Loti than Aziyadé, the woman. 'If this one hadn't been the heroine of his sentiments, another would certainly have been because Loti was ready to link himself with the first woman who would present herself to him: "Yet if she didn't come . . . one of these days another would take her place." '[32]

The Occidental hero is rarely involved in any but a sensual relationship with his mistress. Sex, maid-service, vanity-fulfilment, and occasionally, dependency provide the *raisons d'être* for liaisons, but only in *Aziyadé* does the male character purport to love his mistress.[33] Even here, words of love are couched in cautious terminology, with the stress laid on Aziyadé's affection for Loti. Their association is invoked as 'ce rêve d'amour'[34] and the hero inquires paradoxically how one can separate 'that which comes from the senses from that which comes from the heart'.[35] Only twice does he admit he loves her – the first time almost apologetically: 'the most singular [aspect] of this story is still this: that I love her . . . From the deepest aspect of my being, I love and adore her.'[36] Furthermore, the only other time he claims to love Aziyadé, he qualifies this statement by indicating that his love notwithstanding, he is about to leave her, never to return. 'I was everything for her, the only one she had loved, and the only one who had ever loved her, and I was going to leave her never to return.'[37] If Loti did indeed fall in love with anything, it was with his own fictive creation.[38]

In *Fantôme d'orient*, Loti's eulogy to the Aziyadé affair, Loti is as nostalgic about Stamboul as he is about his love for the young Circassian girl. In a long series of Proustian reminiscences evoking his past feelings for Aziyadé, he synaesthetically links her person with his impressions of Eyub and various sites and sounds of Turkey, ending with the question: 'And above all, why does one feel these strange shocks of recall only in conjunction with the country, places, or time that love has touched with her ring of delicious and mortal magic?'[39] Here Aziyadé is remembered in context only – not as a loved one whose being pervades him even in her absence, but as a figure felt 'only in conjunction with the country, places, or time'. As though to emphasise the Circassian girl's nonexistence, Loti relates an obsessive, recurring dream which has haunted him, presumably weekly, for ten years – but his memories and remembrances are only of the city with which he associates his past love – never of her.

In this obsessive dream which has come back to me so many

times over these ten years, which has come back every week, never, never did I see her young face again, either disfigured or dead; I never obtained, were it of a phantom, the slightest indication, no matter how confused it might have been, of her destiny.[40]

In *Les Désenchantées* Loti describes a similar phenomenon. He returns to the cemetery to find Nedjibé's[41] tomb, and he is thrilled to find the stela there, for he is now realising the fulfilment of a dream.

For years, in the course of his voyages and the restlessness of his errant existence, even to the end of the world, he had dreamed in his sleepless nights so many times of that which resembled the infeasible tasks of bad dreams: in the middle of a sacred cemetery in Stamboul, to lift up again these humble marble stones which were disintegrating.[42]

While the associations with the loved one are weak, those of the cemetery, the tomb, and the city in which the events linked with the beloved took place are strong. Loti is clearly more comfortable with objects and places then he is with people. His recollections of Constantinople, for example, are powerful, and he is capable of graphically conjuring up the presence of this city in all its multiplicitous glory.[43] It is as though the memory of Aziyadé/Nedjibé serves as a key to remembrance of things Turkish, and her presence serves as a touchstone for the *place* in which he met her, rather than her person. Loti seeks Aziyadé and her traces, but in so doing, he lingers long and lovingly over descriptions of the city, its inhabitants, its landscape, and the effect all the reminiscences have upon him.

Similarly, the ambiance and the physical setting have a greater effect on Jean Peyral than do his feelings for Fatou-gaye.

It was three years since Jean Peyral had laid foot on this African earth, and since he was there, a great change had taken place in him. He had passed through several moral phases: the surroundings, the climate, nature had exercised little by little on his young head all their enervating influences; slowly he felt himself slipping down unknown slopes; and today he was the lover of Fatou-gaye, a young black girl from the Khassonkée race, who had thrown on him I don't know what sensual and impure seduction, I don't know what amulet charm.[44]

The devaluation of the importance of women in comparison to the impact of the surroundings is evident in each of the 'Oriental' novels. Loti's final 'tribute' to Madame Chrysanthème is expressed in the following words:

> I took you to have a fling; perhaps you weren't very successful, but you gave what you could, your little person, your curtsies, and your little music; in sum, you were dainty enough in your nippon way. And who knows, perhaps I will think of you sometimes, indirectly, when I remember this beautiful summer, these pretty gardens, and the concert of all these crickets.[45]

In this condescending statement, the association of his 'wife' with summer, gardens, and insect noises, and then only in a secondary capacity, confirms the relative unimportance of the Oriental woman to Loti in comparison to her environment.

The exaltation of the exotic locale at the expense of those who live there reflects Loti's personal biases as well.

> Oceania is a beautiful country; Tahitian women are beautiful creatures; no Grecian regularity in their features, but an original beauty which pleases more. . . . In the end, incomplete women whom one loves like beautiful fruits, fresh water and lovely flowers.[46]

Here the 'incomplete women' are valued no more than the 'beautiful fruits', 'fresh water', and 'pretty flowers' with which they co-exist on the island.

Loti's prejudices are particularly apparent in his discussions of Japan. Of all the countries he visited, Japan, and the Japanese women in particular, suffered the most from his prejudgement. This is obvious when one contrasts the discussion of the sociological realities in Chapter 3 with Loti's descriptions in all his works dealing with this country. Loti cannot contain his contempt for Madame Chrysanthème, which erupts periodically throughout the text when he compares the young woman to various creatures or inanimate objects: 'plaything' (p. 72), 'dog' (p. 92), 'cat' (p. 202), 'doll' (p. 229), and 'insect' (p. 245). Her function as an amusement instead of a thinking, feeling human being serves to dehumanise her. Furthermore, he disparages all her thoughts and actions. When he first moves in with her, he states: 'What can take place in her little head? What I know of her language is still insufficient to find out. Besides, I'll bet one hundred to one that nothing takes place there. – And even if it did, I wouldn't care!'[47] This patronising attitude, which continues throughout the relationship, is never meliorated, even when Loti eventually departs.

Loti's impressions of Japan were first documented in diary form and came to be known as the 'Journal de Nagasaki'. In comparing the 'Journal' with *Madame Chrysanthème*, a Japanese scholar points out that there is a fairly close correlation between the two manuscripts, but that there were several fictional scenes added to the novel 'to place in relief the strangeness and exoticism of this country'.[48] He concludes that Loti never attempted to portray an objective account of Japan, but wanted to infuse his poetic sensibilities into the work, thereby rendering Japanese reality 'personal' and 'instinctive'. 'We find in this book perfectly erroneous conceptions of Japan, [those] of a too accentuated exoticism, of Occidental preconceptions which are no longer valid.'[49] Another Japanese observer also criticised the French novelist for filtering his impressions of Japan through his Occidental lenses to arrive at a conclusion already formulated before he ever left France. 'What he searched for in Japan were the images of Japan that he formed before coming there.'[50]

These conclusions are equally valid for Loti's discussions of Tahiti, Africa and Turkey.[51] The Frenchman usually describes what he sees more or less accurately, but then interprets his finds idiosyncratically. 'He saw each country subjectively, as it affected himself.'[52] This is certainly not unusual in a novelistic vision; what distinguishes Loti from other fictional writers is that he purports to render a realistic, sociologically valid portrait of the areas he is describing. In *Le Mariage de Loti*, for example, he includes factual material (the descriptions of Queen Pomaré and her court are supposedly accurate, as well as those of Queen Vaékéhu, Queen of Nuku-Hiva, the largest of the French Marquesas Islands), realistic delineations of the landscape, and long digressions on Tahitian language, customs, and culture. Thus the reader may assume that the experiences are autobiographical and that the author's conclusions have a valid anthropological basis. This reassurance influences the reader's reaction to Loti's treatment of Oriental women.

Since the description of the setting appears to be realistic, one concludes that the characterisations of the women are also accurate. The reader is exposed to uncomplimentary references to feminine thought processes,[53] and the frequent use of the adjective 'sauvage' to describe Tahitian women points up their uncivilised state. Similarly, when Rarahu asks Loti what he is thinking and he responds: 'Many things . . . that you cannot understand',[54] the reader infers negative conclusions not only about Rarahu alone, but about Rarahu as representative of Tahitian women. We are meant to assume that these remarks offer objective insights into this exotic culture.

Although the implied criticisms of Oriental women are abundant, occasionally Loti recognises that these heroines can be sensible and intelligent. Queen Pomaré of Tahiti, a generally acknowledged enlightened monarch, is described as 'très intelligente et sensée'.[55] Aziyadé has an old friend, Behidjé-hanum, with whom she is very close. This aged woman, who does not permit infidels in her presence, imparts wisdom to her young friend. Every time Aziyadé expresses a new or profound idea, particularly on a subject about which Loti assumes she is ignorant, Aziyadé admits that it is her 'mother', Behidjé, who taught her.[56]

But these instances of enlightened wisdom on the part of women are few and far between, and with the exception of the young, well-educated Turkish women (who have received the benefit of a Western education) in *Les Désenchantées*, the only intelligent women in the Loti Oriental canon are old women. This is because Loti subscribes to the stereotype that wisdom can only be acquired with age, and for that reason beautiful, charming, young women cannot be both attractive and wise.

With his Western eyes, Loti examines and judges both the Oriental woman and her culture. Like his Occidental forebears, he is shocked by the Tahitian culture. When Loti speaks of the effects of missionary activity on the South Seas Islands, he reports that their favourable influence extends only to a presumed absence of cannibalism; 'the superficial Christianity of the natives has not affected their manner of living and the dissoluteness of their mores exceeds any imaginings'.[57] He does present his findings, but he passes moral judgement on the culture as well. Often this implicit condemnation of life or customs in the foreign land is linked somehow to a denunciation of the women in that society. In speaking of Chrysanthème's Buddhism he states:

> Her religion is a shadowy chaos of theogonies, old as the world, held in respect for things very old and more recent ideas on the final, happy nothingness brought from India in the time of our Middle Ages by sacred Chinese missionaries. The Buddhist priests themselves can't make head or tail or it – so what can become of all that grafted in childishness and bird-like flightiness in a sleeping 'mousmé'?[58]

Loti's penchant for revealing his biases is never more apparent than when he writes about Japan. As he becomes more accustomed to life there, he states: 'I even lose my Occidental preconceptions'[59] in a candid admission of prejudice.

The Oriental women, then, are victimised by Loti's 'Orientalist' mentality, and they suffer from his phallocentric preconceptions. They are all defined by denigration; their actions are compared to those of animals, the adjectives used to describe the women are mainly derisive. Like Rarahu, Fatou-gaye also possesses a passionate and ardent nature. She is a 'mixture of young girl, child and black imp, [a] very bizarre urchin'.[60] Fatou's head is 'tousled as a black sheep',[61] and is 'clever as that of a young monkey'.[62] When she dresses her hair in the complicated coiffure of the current mode, she uses bits of straw and twigs covered with a layer of gum which make her appear like a 'porcupine'.[63] 'She was always clean like a black cat dressed in white',[64] and her hands remind Jean of 'monkey paws'.[65] Jean even nicknames her 'yolof', which means 'little monkey girl'.[66] This young 'creature' (p. 126), half slave and half captive, is a true odalisk (p. 136). Although she lives with Jean Peyral, he is unsure of his feelings for her.

> Did Jean love Fatou-gaye? He didn't really know, the poor spahi. He considered her, besides, as an inferior being, a bit like his yellow *laobé* (dog) [author's italics]; he scarcely thought to unravel what there could be at the bottom of this little black soul, black, – black like its Khassonkée envelope.[67]

Jean Peyral's assessment of his little black mistress reflects

Loti's attitude toward Oriental women. Although African society sustains the concept of female inferiority (see Chapter 3), Loti exaggerates the disadvantaged position of women, and in so doing, casts aspersions on Sudanese customs.

> In all the countries of the Sudan, the woman is placed, *vis-à-vis* the man, in a condition of great inferiority. Several times during her life she is bought and sold again like a head of cattle, at a price which diminishes in inverse proportion to her ugliness, her defects and her age.[68]

Moreover, Loti's portrait of Fatou-gaye, replete with continual bestial analogies, reinforces and accentuates the woman's subordinate posture.

Loti cannot dignify Fatou with personal magnetism or even sexual finesse as a reason for Jean's refusal to leave her. Even magic, rather than the young woman's charms, is suggested: 'But was this the power of amulets, – or by dint of habit, – or the inertia of his will ensnared by all the weight of the air? Fatou continued to hold him under her small hand, – and he did not chase her away at all.'[69]

Aziyadé, too, is presumably representative of Moslem women, and Loti's fictional creation is portrayed as vapid and concerned only with her appearance.

> She considers these little hairs [which peek out stubbornly from her coiffure] as indecorous and [she] takes one hour every morning to try to straighten them – without success. This task and polishing her nails red-orange are her two principal occupations.[70]

Not only is her 'occupation' trivialised, but so is her spiritual life. The French author portrays her as being aware of her inferiority to men. During her first conversation with Loti (as translated by Samuel), Aziyadé says '"that her God is not the same as yours, and that she is not sure, according to the Koran, that women have a soul like men [do]"'.[71] This misconception, 'that women, half of humanity, have no souls',[72] was first promulgated in the West by writers and dramatists in Elizabethan times. By placing words of doubt about her immortality in Aziyadé's mouth, Loti continues the gender-inflected, anti-feminist Western literary tradition. It is unlikely that a Moslem woman would really have voiced them, particularly since the Koran specifically includes virtuous women as participants in the rewards of Paradise.[73] Thus, Loti continues to perpetuate a dangerous and erroneous myth which presents Moslem women as inferior to men.

Moslem women are not the only targets of Loti's phallocentrism. Japanese, Tahitian, and African women are all depicted as subservient to the men with whom they live. In addition to the recurrent bestial analogies already mentioned, the author delights in pointing out that the women with whom he (or his protagonist) form relationships are primarily diversions. 'I took her to amuse myself,'[74] he states in *Madame Chrysanthème*. This hedonistic philosophy is echoed in *Aziyadé* when the narrator proclaims: 'I have come to think that everything which pleases me is good to do, and that one should always spice to the utmost the tasteless meal of life.'[75]

Aziyadé, Rarahu, and Fatou-gaye are victimised by Loti or his male protagonist through either physical or psychological mistreatment. The women are used as diversions, to ward off ennui, or to gain insights into their native land. As soon as the objective of the male is attained, the woman is abandoned or destroyed. Rarahu, Fatou-gaye, Aziyadé, and Djénane all succumb when their lovers leave them or die. Only the Japanese women survive their inter-cultural experience with an Occidental, but this is due to the financial rather than the emotional investment on which the association is based. Madame Chrysanthème was hired to fulfil a purpose, which both participants in the scheme recognised. Loti's final images of the mousmé are of her playing with the piastres he gave her, and of her prostrating herself on the threshold of their abode as he departs.

Women, then, are used as ego-supplements to enhance Loti's self-image as well as to advertise his importance to his Occidental readers. Not only do his mistresses worship him, but his purchased females, too, inevitably feel some emotion for him. Loti cannot admit to his readers or to himself that Oriental women might regard the Occidental male with a sentiment other than adoration approaching hero-worship.

Women are also exploited in other ways by Loti. Sometimes he uses them to mask an enterprise which might have unsavoury implications for his reader. By Loti's focusing on heterosexual relations, for example, homosexual innunendoes or exploits are camouflaged, so that the reader tends to repress the debauchery and concentrate on the more socially acceptable (though still exotic) interactions.

Loti's 'tasteless meal of life' seems to have been particularly 'spiced' in *Aziyadé*, where we find intimated hidden depths of sensuality which conflict sharply with the hero's professed love for the heroine, both as individual and as woman. As Barthes has aptly stated: '*Aziyadé* is not a totally rosy book. This novel of a young girl is also a small sodomite epic, marked with allusions to something unheard of and shadowy.'[76] Young Samuel, Loti's servant and go-between in arranging for Aziyadé's rendezvous with her lover, is strangely devoted to his employer. One evening when the two men were lying outside together to escape the June heat, Samuel was particularly ill-humoured. The hero asked:

'Aren't you happy with me? And what have I done to you?' His hand trembled in mine and clasped it more than would have been necessary. – *Che volete*, said he in a sombre and troubled voice, *che volete mi*? (What do you want from me?) Something unheard of and sinister had passed for a moment through poor Samuel's head; in the old Orient, anything is possible. . . . Since this strange instance, he is at my service body and soul.[77]

Samuel and Achmet, the protagonist's two friends and faithful servants, share his thoughts and Turkish experiences well beyond the appropriate confines of a master-servant relationship.

My evenings passed in the company of Samuel. I saw strange things with him in the boatmen's taverns. . . . Little by little I became attached to him, and his refusal to serve me by Aziyadé's side made me value him more. . . . But I have seen strange things [in] the night with this vagabond, a strange prostitution in the caves where one drinks mastic and raki into complete intoxication.[78]

Achmet, Aziyadé's chief support and attendant, generally pleads with Loti on her behalf. But even his association with Aziyadé is suspect, as he is willing to do anything and go anywhere just to serve his Occidental-turned-Turkish master. To prove his affection for Loti, Achmet refuses to accept any wages and, on the contrary, he is willing to offer his employer half his property in order to prevent him from leaving Stamboul. The last evening of merrymaking after Aziyadé has returned to her husband, Loti and Achmet reappear in their old café to dance and sing with the all-male clientèle. Achmet orders an orchestra to appear, and Loti demands his 'narguilhé' and coffee cup to be brought and refilled every quarter-hour. In the ensuing noise-filled and inebriated gathering

> I no longer saw myself except through a fog, my head was full of strange and incoherent thoughts. The groups, exhausted and breathless, passed and repassed in the obscurity. The dance still whirled, and Achmet, at each turn, broke a window pane with the back of his hand.
>
> One by one, all the windows of the establishment fell to the ground and were pulverised under the feet of the dancers; Achmet's hands, belaboured with deep cuts, bloodied the floor.[79]

The abiding love of both Achmet and Samuel for Loti, manifested by both physical and emotional marks of affection, rivals that of Aziyadé. Not only does this masculine love parallel the feminine (Aziyadé's farewell dance culminates in self-inflicted deep cuts in her arm to prove her undying love for Loti) but Loti exerts his power over the three equally. When Achmet, the go-between, writes to Loti in Europe responding to a letter that the Englishman has written to Aziyadé, the Turk informs his friend of Aziyadé's illness (pining for Loti), but he ends his letter with:

> Loti, the words which you told me, don't forget them; the promises which you made me, never forget them! In your thoughts, do you believe that I can be happy one single moment without you in Constantinople? I cannot, and when you left, my heart broke with grief.[80]

Although Loti reports his strong feelings of love for Aziyadé based, of course, on the mutuality of her response,[81] the continued references to Samuel and Achmet's devotion to him serve to rupture the notion of an idyllic, conventional romance. Loti maintained in his autobiography that his self-respect prevented him from engaging in 'la débauche vulgaire',[82] but the frequent allusions to 'la pâle débauche' in *Aziyadé*, as well as the several scenes depicting various nocturnal expeditions and all-male parties with his friend Izeddin-Ali (pp. 68–9, Chapter LIV) belie the strong heterosexual attachment Loti presumably professes, and point, minimally, to a yearning for another kind of love. The underground suburban soirées which Loti frequents at the end of a wild night reveal

> young Asian boys, costumed as beggars, [who] executed lascivious dances before a public composed of all the hardened criminals of Ottoman justice, a saturnalia of a loathsome new invention. I begged out of the end of this spectacle, worthy of the best moments of Sodom.[83]

Loti openly engages in sexual excesses with prostitutes and probably with his servants (although this is never made clear in the text) and Aziyadé is presumably understanding and accepting of her lover's behaviour. 'She didn't doubt, poor little one, that this boy with the youthful face had already abused everything in life, and only brought her a blasé heart, in quest of some original novelty; she told herself that it would be good to be thus loved.'[84] Here Loti not only admits to the 'novelty' of his affairs with his Turkish mistress, but he basks in the fantasy of its sanction by Aziyadé. Further, since he continues to live with her and he has her approval, any possible stigma which might be associated with his 'imprudences' is eliminated.

Sexual adventures are not the only means by which Loti uses Oriental women in this novel. Cruelty and self-interest also motivate the author to manipulate his characters and friends according to his whims. At one point during his affair with Aziyadé, he encounters three beautiful women during a carriage ride, and is instantly attracted to one of them, the courtesan Séniha. Several days later, Loti decides that he must have Séniha, and toward that end, he tells Aziyadé that she must leave.

> I had told her that I didn't want her around any more as of the next day; that another was going to take her place for a few days; that she, herself, would come back again afterward, and that she would still love me after this humiliation without even remembering it.[85]

Once again Loti luxuriates in the control he exercises over his friends despite his insensitivity and his callousness. No matter what injustice the Frenchman perpetrates on Aziyadé and faithful Achmet, they return to Loti's quarters after he satisfies his curiosity with this adventure. Séniha, too, complies with Loti's demands; she arrives at his beckoning and leaves as soon as he demands it, making no mention of Loti's strange behaviour. The Séniha incident also raises questions in the reader's mind; why should the hero experience such a strong revulsion for a woman toward whom he presumably entertains a strong, physical attraction? And why does she leave so docilely, without making any reproaches to her host?[86] Once again the male fantasy creates a situation wherein the masculine protagonist is able to dominate and assert his power over women, where he is always in command of any situation and able to manipulate any female according to his momentary caprice. Like Aladdin, he need only perform a simple act for his smallest wishes to be realised. And for Loti, not only women but also his male servants (whose feminine characteristics have already been noted) fawn and yield submissively to any request or directive which might suddenly occur to him.

> The devotion of these three Turks is the response he seeks from his friends: it is an affection which gives itself entirely to Loti and does not require anything in return. It is, also, an affection which enhances his importance and the stature of the hero, making him feel like a god in a world where his authority is never questioned and his will is supreme.[87]

In most of the 'Oriental' oeuvre, Loti provides himself or his protagonist with adulating sailor friends in addition to his mistress or 'wife'. These men are unquestioning in their loyalty, and their close friendship with the hero is stressed. They accompany the protagonist on his adventures with women, supporting his liaisons but never interfering with the protagonist's sensual involvement. Even though they remain in the background of a heterosexual affiliation, there are troubling moments in the text which cast doubts on what appears to be the primary relationship in the work. Madame Chrysanthème, Loti's 'wife', provides a front for the hero's affection for his sailor friend, Yves. The only tension in this text is created by the hero's fear that Madame Chrysanthème and Yves might be involved with each other in this 'ménage à trois'. Loti's apprehensions are alleviated when Yves confesses that he could never be interested in Madame Chrysanthème, as she 'belongs' to the protagonist. Loti is more concerned to establish Yves' continued fidelity to him than to determine whether the tall sailor was unfaithful with the little Japanese woman.

> But he [Yves] considers her my wife, and thus [she is] sacred. I believe in his word in the most complete manner possible, and I experience a true relief, a real joy in finding again my brave Yves of yore. How was I able to submit to such a demeaning influence from the surroundings as to suspect him and to make myself suffer such a petty wrong?
> Let us never speak of this doll again . . .[88]

The filial bond established between Loti and a French sailor friend is repeated in almost every novel.[89] Plumkett, Loti's first fictive confidant, appears initially in *Aziyadé*: 'There are few people with whom this boy,' Loti writes about himself to Plumkett, 'so withdrawn in disposition, speaks occasionally in a rather intimate manner, – but you are [one] of them.'[90] He provides the intellectual and artistic guidance and kinship which Loti cannot find in his Turkish friends. Plumkett, who is more ascetic than Loti, writes him long letters in which he expresses his sentiments as more elevated and longer-lasting then any purely emotional (that is, heterosexual) ones.

> What happiness to be able to say everything one feels to someone who understands *completely* and not only *up to a certain point* [author's italics], to someone who finishes your thought with the same word which was on your lips, whose reply makes a torrent of conceptions and a flood of ideas gush forth. . . . You are two intelligences who add to one another and complete one another.[91]

Nowhere in the entire Loti Oriental canon can one find such a reciprocal heterosexual relationship; on the contrary, close masculine friendship is employed as a foil against which the Loti protagonist conducts his liaison with his non-Occidental paramour.

In *Le Mariage de Loti*, Plumkett (now with the Christian name, John) reappears; he has the same name but a different personality.

This is true of Loti as well. The blasé, decadent Loti/Arif Bey of the first publication has given way to a more ingenuous, newly baptised Harry Grant, whose name, Loti, derives from his Polynesian playmates. John, like so many of Loti's sailor friends, 'is not like me . . . moreover, he is still the same true and blameless friend, this same good and tender brother who watches over me like a guardian angel and whom I love wholeheartedly'.[92] Regardless of Loti's actions, John remains loyal and supportive of his shipmate, whose new relationship with Rarahu seems to have supplanted their old, close ties.

Although the nature of the Loti/Plumkett friendship is never articulated, enigmatic comments sprinkled throughout the text cause speculation. Phrases like: 'John . . . my beloved brother, John . . . sustained a pained surprise when he was told of my nocturnal walks in the company of Faimana' and 'he was ready to pardon his brother Harry for anything when it came to her',[93] or 'John, my brother John, passes in the middle of those festivities like a handsome mystical figure, inexplicable for the Tahitian women who would never find the path to his heart, nor the vulnerable side of his neophyte purity'[94] are pregnant with allusion. Why should John feel the need to 'forgive' his 'brother' for Harry's new-found friendship with Rarahu, and why would the Tahitian ladies 'never find the path to his heart'? These gratuitous remarks, which have no bearing on the action and are too cryptic to serve as character development, must have been placed in the text for a purpose. It appears as though the South Seas episode disguises a less conventional relationship between John and Harry Grant. Loti's hints concerning alternative sexual attractions emerge almost in spite of himself. It appears as though he cannot fully suppress the evidence or that, in his candour, he intimates the truth without explicitly revealing it.

Plumkett resurfaces again as Loti's correspondent and confidant in *Fleurs d'ennui*. In this work he emerges as the second participant in the dialogue which forms the frame for the several stories in the volume. Like Loti, he suffers from ennui, but he is more sophisticated and more philosophical than his epistolary friend. In 'Suleima' he also appears as a character. When Loti first meets the young prostitute, he is with Plumkett, and he declines her implicit invitation ('And then she continues to laugh – and this very particular laugh clearly bespeaks the nasty career which she has already begun to undertake'[95]) in favour of a wild horseback rise with his friend. Interestingly, the horseback ride, a symbol of passion in nineteenth-century literature, usually associated with female characters to identify the unspoken, is here inverted to encompass Loti and his male friend.

Upon their return, he sees Suleima again, and she personifies for him the sensuality of the Orient – the great 'warm and free life' which beckons and attracts him. He desires her, 'yet modesty holds me back, above all before Plumkett; he always sees, too clearly, everything which I should like to hide. And then, those kinds of love which one must submit to, confound me and make me doubt all'.[96] The interesting element in this passage is that Loti would feel inhibited before his fellow sailor during their limited port stay, and that he should use the word *subir* (submit) to describe the heterosexual relationship about which he feels so ambivalent. One wonders about the special hold Plumkett has on his friend which would prevent Loti from heeding Suleima's appeal.

In these novels, Loti or his protagonist are always attracted to women; his friend or confidant either sanctions or condemns the hero's behaviour, but he is rarely involved with a woman himself. Loti seems to require acceptance of his feelings or conduct by his naval brethren, who also validate his power over others. The seamen's fictive rôle is also curious, as they rarely serve to forward the plot action but act instead as conscience or patient companion to Loti's more wayward and sensually experimental personality.

In *Les Désenchantées*, Jean Renaud, a young friend from the Embassy, provides the Occidental support which Lhéry needs to encounter the three 'veiled shadows'. Renaud serves as a silent accomplice during several rendezvous, but what is remarkable is that Mélek senses that he is a 'hostile influence' against the three women.[97] Why Jean Renaud would disapprove of these three women is left obscure, but it is certainly worthwhile considering that he might have felt his relationship with Loti threatened. The nature of that relationship is, as usual, never made explicit, and the Platonic association with the three women might provide a cover for Loti's affiliation with the younger man.

Loti, then, uses women to mask perverse or socially unacceptable liaisons. To justify the feminine characters' secondary status, the author sometimes ascribes undesirable character traits to the Oriental women which, in turn, provoke violent reactions from the male hero. Sometimes the defects are those of omission – the female is too passive, too stupid, or too dependent and Loti (or his protagonist) punish her by inciting physical or mental abuse. In *Le Roman d'un spahi*, the female victim returns to the male aggressor despite his violence. When Jean Peyral discovers that his black mistress, Fatou-gaye, has sold his watch, an heirloom given him by his father prior to the spahi's departure, he is so enraged that he beats her with his riding crop.

> Jean did not feel his strength in these moments of fury. He was possessed of these quite savage violent feelings, a bit like children grown up in the wild. He struck severely Fatou's naked back, marking the stripes from whence the blood gushes forth and his rage was aroused as he hit.[98]

This first taste of sadistic rage is followed by subsequent beatings. Jean's ardour is no longer aroused by Fatou's femininity; beatings alone satisfy him, for he is repulsed by her 'blackness', her 'perversity', and her 'wickedness'.[99]

Loti now converts this sadism into masochism. Instead of feeling horror for Jean's act, Fatou is shown as countenancing his violence. 'When he beat her, she almost loved it now, because it was only during those moments that he touched her, and that she could touch him, herself, in pressing herself against him to ask for forgiveness.'[100] By creating women who acquiesce to torment by a male, Loti justifies and rationalises his protagonists' mistreatment of women.

Brutality appears in mental as well as physical guise. In *Le Mariage de Loti*, Ariitéa, one of Queen Pomaré's ladies-in-waiting, is very attractive to Loti. Although he lives with Rarahu and is clearly her lover, he frequently mentions Ariitéa to her, and indicates openly on several occasions that he would enjoy Ariitéa's company. During a major festival on the Isle of Mooréa, to which the Queen's court and her retinue are invited, members of Loti's ship, the *Rendeer*, are also included. In the midst of the joyous activities, Loti states:

> I had been summoned by Ariitéa to keep her company during this official lunch, – and poor little Rarahu, who had only come because of me, waited for me a long time on the bridge, crying in silence to see herself thus abandoned. Very severe punishment

which I had inflicted upon her, for a childlike caprice which
lasted from the evening before and had already made her shed
tears.[101]

The 'caprice d'enfant' to which Loti alludes is nowhere clarified in
the text. Here the male power figure exerts his authority through
'punishment' and 'abandonment', and seems to revel in the
negative effect this produces on his mistress.

Sometimes Loti, both as author and protagonist, seems
unconscious of the consequences of his self-centredness, and
seems incapable of projecting the effects of his words on another
human being. In *Un Jeune Officier pauvre*, Loti reproduces a letter
he supposedly wrote to Aziyadé in response to her appeal to help
her escape from Turkey.[102] He counsels her to remain with her
present husband, but if he dies, he tells her to marry Osman
Effendi, a rich, young man who loves her and will make her
happy.

Forget Loti, who brings unhappiness to those who approach
him. With Osman Effendi you will have slaves, gardens, a
position among women of your country and your place of wife
in the invisible world of harems.

While with me! Even if all the impossibilities were conquered,
have you thought of what it would be like to be my wife? To
come alone, as fugitive, into a distant country where no one
would understand your tongue . . . To go without veil, a
'Frankish' woman; to share my misery, to attend to difficult
housework like your servants do and, during the years when I
will be far away, travelling on the high seas, to remain alone.
During long winters, longer than those in Constantinople, in
this country further removed from the cold star, to never see
either blue sky or your country, or your countrymen, nor to
ever again hear a friend's voice . . .

But if you accept all that, my beloved, *if you love me so much
that you would be willing to endure all that* [author's italics], if you
want to flee . . . then come, I adore you and I await you.[103]

This back-handed invitation to join Loti could only be construed
adversely by any self-respecting woman. Here the Frenchman
offers himself only as the least appealing alternative of many. He
phrases his proposal in such negative terms that he demeans the

woman to whom he writes, simultaneously assuring her refusal. The overt statements point to Loti's entreaties to come to France and join him, but the subtext, the true message, negates that request and ensures that Aziyadé remain in Turkey. The continual dialectic between the stated remark and its implied opposition deconstructs the comment and marks another of Loti's techniques for exploiting women.

This approach in discussing women is habitual; Loti makes a socially acceptable statement or a seemingly favourable comparison, and then undercuts the compliment by presenting the alternative more desirably, or by following the flattery with uncomplimentary statements. Thus the reader is invited to simultaneously accept and then reject the author's attempt at a positive portrait of Oriental women. Again and again Loti's implied criticism superposes the initial remark. 'Yes, seen from behind, they are adorable; they have, like all Japanese women, small, delicious napes. In speaking of them, we say: "Our little performing dogs", and in truth they are singularly like them.'[104] It is difficult to admire these 'adorable' Japanese women when the context in which they operate is that of 'performing dogs'.

When Loti first meets the mousmé April-Shower in *Mme Prune*, he finds her 'strange', 'half doll and half cat', 'amazing, unlike anything else, indefinable, and sexless'. This young thirteen-year-old child attracts him through her 'bizarrerie', her dancing, and her dramatic abilities. The various masks she employs in her art form intrigue him, but what enchants him most is that 'I have met the plaything which I had, vaguely perhaps, desired all my life: a little talking cat'.[105] Although Loti's love for cats was proverbial, this analogy of a woman to both the animal and a toy can only be denigrating.

Not only did the French author delight in comparing women to animals and inanimate objects, but he even portrayed Oriental women as ignorant of the true implications of these invidious comparisons. Thus, the females are made to appear senseless. When Fatou is repeatedly compared to a monkey, she finally rebels when Jean says: 'You are the same thing as a monkey', and retorts: *'Ah Tjean! Don't say that, my white man! First of all a monkey doesn't know how to speak, – and I do very well!'*[106] [author's italics]. Fatou-gaye's 'revolt' continues the gender-inflected tradition in which Loti conceives her intellect. Fatou doesn't object to being called a 'thing' and only resents the beastly comparison because she perceives speech to be the distinguishing factor between herself and the animal.

Even death does not terminate Loti's opportunities to manipulate women. The many trips to the loved one's graveside, the several eulogies to her memory all have as their object the author's self-aggrandisement. As Loti mourns he suffers, and his suffering consumes him with self-pity, one of his favourite sentiments. The compassion he feels for the dead is based on sorrow for *his* loss and fear that his own mortality is now invoked. In addition, he uses his necrophilic tendencies to obfuscate perfectly valid feelings of grief toward his old Turkish servant friend. *Fantôme d'orient* ostensibly deals with Loti's search for Aziyadé, but the Frenchman does not fail to visit the Christian cemetery in which Achmet was buried. The desolate nature of the area with its few wooden and stone crosses, empty of any vegetation contrasts sharply with the larger, more densely filled Muslim cemetery in which Aziyadé is interred. The reactions he feels toward his former friends is also curious. As he is first led to Aziyadé's tomb he states: 'But how is it that I became again suddenly so calm, almost absent-minded? It seems that I don't understand well any more, that I am no longer here. Who then has closed my heart in such an unexpected manner?'[107]

Loti does revisit Aziyadé's tomb, there to lie on her grave, embrace the earth, and give her a final farewell kiss. As he lies there, overcome by the funereal aspect of the cemetery, 'I become conscious again, little by little, of things; I suffer more simply, I understand in a more human and more painful manner, the shudder comes back again to me, the true shudder of infinite sadness.'[108]

Here Loti wallows in self-pity, one of his favourite maudlin pleasures. Nothing pleases him more than to contemplate death and the sadness of leaving life, and particularly as he grows older, he seizes upon any and every opportunity to declaim on its meaning:

When we die, it is only the beginning of a series of other partial destructions, plunging us always further into absolute black night. Those who loved us also die thus; all human heads in which our image was semi-conserved, break up and return to dust; everything which belonged to us disperses and crumbles away; our portraits, which no one knows anymore, become obliterated; – and our name is forgotten.[109]

What is interesting about this quotation is its self-absorbed quality; the rumination about death has less to do with philosophical anxiety about the unknown or a desire to come to terms with absolute finality than it does with the implication of Loti's future immortality. He fears death because his worldly possessions and his pictures will disintegrate and no one will remember his name. Aziyadé's death creates a strong impression upon his thoughts because she remembered *him*, and thus assured him temporary immortality. Regret for his former mistress is more a question of regret for himself and his life than it is sorrow for her departure. Thus, although he seeks his past love, one is struck by the egocentric aspects of the quest. It is *his* sadness, *his* suffering, *his* nostalgia which is paramount. 'How to speak of the charm of this place called the Golden Horn! How to speak of it even slightly: it is composed of my uneasy joys and of my anguish, mixed in the shadow of Islam; undoubtedly, it only exists for me alone.'[110] This sollipsism accounts for Loti's need to portray all the women with whom he forms relationships as being dependent upon him and as being unable to function effectively once he or his male protagonist has left them.

In *Les Désenchantées*, Loti expresses similar sentiments as he visits Hakidjé's tomb, but here the emphasis is on his thoughts as providing the final link between his former mistress's memory and obscurity. As André Lhéry (Loti's fictive counterpart) walks through the cemetery, he speculates that none but he still remembers his beloved. 'In his singular memory, but none other, the young image still persisted and, when he would be dead, no reflection of what had been her beauty would remain any more, no worldly trace of what had been her anxious and candid soul.'[111] In this case, Loti congratulates himself upon having written a previous (but unnamed book) about this woman, as the work will immortalise her and continue to arouse compassion for her among generations of Turkish women. Once again, Loti becomes the conduit for eternalisation of a woman's posthumous fame; the focus of the passage is as much on Loti's abilities to preserve the dead girl's memory as it is on the victim's attributes. Thus Loti uses women, even in death, to celebrate and to concentrate attention upon himself and his abilities.

In summary, then, Loti uses Oriental women primarily to enhance his sense of self. By depicting the Occidental hero as omnipotent *vis-à-vis* his worshipful Oriental paramour, by creating women who are so dependent on their lovers that they die or commit suicide when they are abandoned, by portraying men as always controlling the relationship, Loti creates a male fantasy world in which all his (or his heroes') inadequacies are nullified. Furthermore, he appeals to the Occidental reader who perceives himself as superior to the foreign civilisation whose culture is different from (and thus considered inferior to) his own. Social and political realities notwithstanding, Loti reflects the general nineteenth-century French views on women and the Orient, but exaggerated by his own peculiar concerns and unease.

6

The Exploiter Exploited

Of all Loti's novels, *Les Désenchantées* has provoked the least critical attention, although much has been written about it. While this book is very different in tone from his other Oriental works, no satisfactory explanation has ever been given for Loti's new perspective on Oriental women. Whereas Rarahu, Fatou-gaye, and Aziyadé were dependent, passive, and primitive females living in the shadow of their European hero, the three 'Turkish' women who comprised 'Nour el Nissa' were strong, intelligent, highly educated, articulate young ladies, very sure of themselves and their mission in life. Unlike their non-Occidental consoeurs who needed men to exist, these women chronicled their despair at having to survive in a male-oriented society where men caused them only unhappiness and, ultimately, death. Since this work is so exceptional in the Oriental oeuvre, and since the feminine figures portrayed are unlike those in any previous characterisation, it seems pertinent to inquire why Loti would suddenly create a new image for the Oriental woman, and what motivated him to write this book.

Loti took great pains to plead for more social equality for Turkish women, whom he depicted as victimised by their society. Thus *Les Désenchantées* is the most pro-feminine book he ever wrote. It represents a milestone in feminist thought for the early twentieth century because it pleads for equal rights for women at a time when they were mostly regarded as second-class citizens.

Nevertheless, there is still a conflict in the text between his essentially sympathetic, though condescending, attitudes towards women and the actual fate of his heroines, whose symbolic plight served his didactic purpose. On the one hand, Loti presents the women as perceptive and conscious of their situation as second-class citizens in a patriarchal society, on the other hand he undermines this position by patronising them. He attributes a 'disordered flight' of mind to his heroine, Djénane[1] and speaks of her as a 'little barbarian princess' (p. 37). Although he finds the voices of his three 'veiled phantoms' pleasing, he admits that 'three women from the Pera section of Stamboul speaking together, would make one think instantly of the cockatoo section in the zoo'.[2] All three women either die or contain 'the seeds of death'[3] within them – a heavy price to pay for self-assertion in the male world. Whether married or single, these women are not permitted to function without men and when they try to assert their independence, they succumb.

One critic objected to this portrayal of Ottoman women. Mme Rachilde faults Loti for his sexist position in this novel, for feeling the need to describe women as requiring men in order to exist and be happy.

The secret disenchantment of women in a harem or outside [one] is to dream of a eunuch before a male, if they do not sigh for a male before the eunuchs. Little Djénane, of course, is no exception to this, and she ends up by killing herself, so weary of embracing only the wind. Peace to your ashes little silly! In France one is less a bazaar doll than you, and we read our great writers without losing our heads![4]

For other critics, no such troublesome spots existed in the text. Idiosyncratic readings aside,[5] most critics have contented themselves with recapitulating the plot and the circumstances surrounding the invention of *Les Déscenchantées* (for example, Briquet, *Pierre Loti et l'orient*, Robert Poulet, 'Pierre Loti, enchanteur désenchanté', Michael Lerner, *Pierre Loti*), or have dismissed it as 'tedious' and 'lifeless' without attempting to analyse it (Clive Wake, *The Novels of Pierre Loti*). Two contemporary critics, Jules Bois in *Les Annales*, 29 July 1906, and Victor Giraud in *La Revue des Deux Mondes*, 1 June 1907, were confused by what motivated Loti to write so differently in this novel from what he had produced before, but neither attempted to interpret his findings. A third critic of the time, André Chaumeix, commented that the women Loti usually depicted were 'small, sensual animals who didn't care about ideas' but in this work, they were 'completely spiritual and he [Loti] seem[ed] to look for and describe something other than the picturesque and the sensual'.[6] Once again, the critic was content to present the evidence without considering the implications of those findings.

No critic, however, has yet explained why the attitudes Loti expresses in this book toward Oriental women are so different

from those expressed in Loti's previous oeuvre. Many
commentators have discussed the influence of Marc Hélys, Loti's
plot originator, on the gestation of the novel, and commented on
the sailor/author's gullibility. But describing the situation in no
way explains it, and even Raymonde Lefèvre in her lengthy study
of *Les Désenchantées* was finally unable to explicate the reasons for
the pro-feminine views in a writer who, as we have seen, was
ordinarily sexist in his approach toward the Oriental woman.
Claude Farrère complained that 'he [Loti] did not write his
personal convictions here as witnessed by his own eyes. It isn't
his thought which he delivers to us: it is a second-hand recital, an
argument he listened to and reproduced.'[7] It is my intention, in
this chapter, to explore the reasons why Loti adopted an attitude
toward the Oriental woman different from the one he had
expressed heretofore, and to examine the role that Marc Hélys
and her friends played in this literary 'mystification'.

Marc Hélys[8] was a French writer who had first come to
Constantinople in 1901 when she spent a summer with two
Moslem women friends. She returned in 1904 in order to work,
but this time stayed with a European household because 'my
work demanded more liberty than a Turkish home could offer'.[9]
During her first sojourn, she had made the acquaintance of
several Turkish young ladies, friends and relatives of her upper-
class hostesses, and found that 'with about two or three
exceptions, none possessed general culture, the polish of varied
attainments'.[10]

Her two friends, however, were different. They were half-
French, half-Circassian sisters whose life-style was almost totally
European, and their French father prided himself on having
children who were 'without a drop of Turkish blood'.[11] The two
'Orientals' had been raised in a strange manner – a combination
of 'egoism and absurdity'. They were multilingual (French, Greek,
German, English, Russian and Italian supplemented their Turkish),
musical, and artistic. They were well-grounded in Moslem studies,
and in order to better understand the Koran, they had been
schooled in Arabic and Persian. They had some familiarity with
history, literature, and philosophy, although Marc Hélys
complained of their superficial knowledge in these fields.
However, 'thanks to their lively and supple intelligence, the entire
ensemble made up a mind of extremely brilliant facets'.[12]

These two women, who had been educated to please their

Occidental father, were unhappy in their condition. Their reading matter was undirected and superficial, and they lived in a 'false' world, longing for the Western 'reality' which seemed so far away. They were isolated, and their circle of acquaintances was narrow and not representative of the modern Turkish woman.[13] Marc Hélys complained that she would have enjoyed meeting more Turkish women, but the language barrier prevented her from communicating with them.

During Hélys's second visit in 1904, she found that the life-styles pursued by these upper-class young women was unchanged from those followed three years earlier. There were few diversions and much ennui. Whether married, divorced, or single, all led a dismal existence. They were unhappy, idle, and bored. During that summer, the chief topic of conversation among the Turkish women seems to have been Loti's presence on board the 'Vautour', a ship anchored in the Bosphorus.[14] Marc Hélys and her two Turkish friends wanted a diversion from their monotonous existence, so they decided to write him a letter, with no other initial aim than to make contact with a 'grand personnage', particularly one who was shy and removed from public view.[15] Hiding behind their 'Turkishness', they decided that they could approach him in their veiled costumes, thus remaining totally incognito. Their letter to him would attempt to arrange a rendezvous by seducing him with flattery. Using the excuse of a former letter which Zennour, the married sister, had written two years earlier congratulating him on the publication of *Aziyadé*, Nouryé, Zennour, and Leyla (Marc Hélys) drafted a letter to Loti under the composite name of 'Nour el Nissa'. They invited him to meet them in Tarabiya, a small town on the Bosphorus, not far from Constantinople.

To their surprise, Loti responded, but his answer annoyed them. He was afraid of a hoax (he used the word 'mystification'), but since he had some business in the same town on that very day, and provided '*the weather were good*' (his emphasis) he might pass by the café at the designated time in order not to 'cause you distress, in case this were serious'.[16] This answer irritated the three, who found his conceit 'shocking'. They wanted to teach him a lesson and they wanted to make him an object of ridicule.

On the Saturday in question the famous author met them at the appointed spot and seemed somewhat uncomfortable during their rendezvous. He asked them to remove their veils, but they politely declined, and he never again repeated the request.[17] He was apparently a poor conversationalist: 'Truly we were very surprised. We knew beforehand that Pierre Loti spoke little, but all the same, we didn't expect such a poverty of conversation.'[18]

Loti seemed more anxious to absorb the experience through his eyes and through his memory than through his speech. The women initiated the topics of discussion; he seemed overwhelmed and was definitely at a disadvantage. He was uncomfortable with their veils, which prevented him from seeing either their facial expressions or their eyes. He showed himself to be very sensitive; when two of the women exchanged a few words in Turkish, he informed them that he understood the language sufficiently well so that he would be aware if they exchanged 'on his account some uncivil remark'.[19] In Hélys' opinion, the conversation itself was very inane; the three chatted about some mutual acquaintances, Loti's cat, and about his books. Hélys' flattery ('By scattering yourself in pieces all over the world, little must be left for yourself')[20] elicited the response that it was really in Turkey alone that the greatest part of him remained. And after further inquiry, he offered the information that 'three-fourths' of him was here. As there seemed to be little more to talk about, the women decided to leave, using as a pretext their need to arrive in Stamboul before sundown.

Loti was very affected by the entire experience, and as Nouryé sensed that he wanted to continue the relationship, she suggested that the four meet again. It was because of the depth of emotion which Pierre Loti manifested as he was actually living an adventure, that the project of having Loti *live a novel* was born.

Throughout the ensuing months, the triumvirate planned meetings in different places around Constantinople. Sometimes they would come together in a private home, sometimes in a mosque, sometimes in the cemetery where Hakidjé (Aziyadé) was buried. Their initial aim seems to have been to 'arrange pretty memories for Pierre Loti'.[21] These 'memories' would be based on meetings contrived by the women and letters exchanged between the four participants. Loti would encounter his 'veiled shadows' in different spots in Constantinople; he would try to familiarise himself with their lives and life styles, and they would then mix fact and fantasy in their answers.

Although the exact nature of the subject-matter was not immediately apparent, the women knew that they wanted to play on the older man's emotions: 'I *wanted* Loti moved for these Turkish women. . . . I spoke to him of the novel to be written. Had he *felt* our soul?'[22] 'And Neyr added: "As he cannot invent what he doesn't know himself, we must invent for him." "But in relationship to what he knows," I added. "He must feel and be moved." '[23] On the other hand, they expected to observe Loti's creative powers in motion, and they thought that they would discover how he wrote.

> We wanted to see how he composed his books. We thought that he was going to live a novel, that we would only have to follow and give him a reply. Just the contrary happened. The novel would have been finished right away if we hadn't made the incidents occur. Because he furnished nothing.[24]

Not only was it important to create emotion for the artist, but according to the intriguers, it was also necessary to invent the plot. Loti could carry out his assignments and faithfully record events and his impressions of them, but Hélys and her friends maintained that he would have been incapable of creating the situation which they had provided. In addition, their knowledge of his oeuvre, not to mention their personal acquaintance with him, assured them that he possessed a descriptive rather than analytical mind. Despite his undeniable gift for writing and his evident curiosity in portraying characters, they felt that he was either uninterested or incapable of analysing motivation. Moreover, they gave him little credit for psychological insight. 'And for that book, Pierre Loti needed everything we gave him. With all his genius, he didn't possess the gift of penetrating into other souls.'[25] It is possible, of course, that these remarks were self-serving, and that Hélys was trying to take more credit for the conception of the novel than was really her due. However, the comparison of her letters with the published epistles in *Les Désenchantées* shows such a striking similarity and frequently verbatim transcription, that I think we can safely accept the validity of her assessments.[26]

Loti seemed little more than a marionette in their hands, and he obediently executed their drama. *Les Désenchantées* actually unites two separate stories – one fabricated and one real – both of which were arranged by Marc Hélys: the actual account of the three women's relationship with Pierre Loti and the fictitious narrative which Hélys developed in her correspondence with him. The two plots merge in *Les Désenchantées* when Loti describes in his text several of the real-life encounters which Hélys and her friends consciously arranged to give him a taste of the varied activities Turkish women engaged in and to better depict the 'plight' of the Turkish women (that is, silent meetings in caiques on the Sweet Waters of Asia, clandestine encounters on land, meetings in private homes with other Turkish women). In *Le Secret des Désenchantées*, Hélys separates the fact from the fantasy for us in order

> to help . . . his future biographers and critics to better understand and to clarify his originality . . . [Through my recollections] the reader will be surprised at the lively manner in which Loti writes, the subtle and charming art with which he transforms the elements furnished by reality and [how] he envelops them with dazzling poetry.[27]

Thus, she gives him credit for style and literary ability, if not for invention. Although he embellished upon her original idea and added reminiscences of Aziyadé along with an enlarged profile of himself as male hero, by and large he executed the novel whose plot-line she conceived. The pro-feminine posture which he articulated was her position.

Loti seems to have believed everything his new-found acquaintances told him; as a chiefly impressionistic writer, his style had always been to record his impressions of a place and its people, elaborate the initial information just enough to create an interesting ambiance, and then publish his achievement without resort to historical or journalistic research. Unlike Flaubert or even Balzac, he was uninterested in research and authentic documentation; his five senses were sufficient authority for him. Marc Hélys and her friends knew this, and took advantage of the French author's naiveté.

Because Marc Hélys was such a good judge of character, she was able to dupe Loti thoroughly. She and her friends had clearly taken his measure even before they approached him, and their first letter to him contained words of unexpected candour concerning his treatment of women.

> But in order to become her [the Turkish woman's] friend tomorrow, Loti, you must learn to see in her *something other than*

a nice souvenir of a trip, an enchanted stage in your artistic life in pursuit of new emotions. From now on *she will no longer be for you the child toward whom you leaned nor the mistress easily made happy by the charity of your tenderness* . . . the time has come for you *to look for and paint in love something other than the picturesque.* [my italics][28]

Surprisingly, he was unoffended by their frankness. It may be that Marc Hélys's French background assisted her in appealing to Loti's sensibilities. 'Perhaps because of that, I knew better how to speak of Muslims to a European.'[29] Raymonde Lefêvre comes to a similar conclusion in *La Vie inquiète de Pierre Loti*, asserting that Loti was attracted to Leyla/Djénane precisely because she was Occidental.[30] Although this statement may appear strange in the light of all Loti's previous experiences with Oriental women, the nature of this last relationship was decidedly different from that of any previous one. For Loti treated this modern woman more as an *equal* than he did any of the previous Oriental women in his oeuvre. Furthermore, she resembles the Occidental women the author describes (Gaud in *Pêcheur d'Islands*, the Widow in *Matelot*, and Marie, Yves' wife in *Mon Frère Yves*) far more closely than her Oriental counterparts, for she is a product of a different (higher) class.[31]

And what caused Loti to respond so favourably to the Frenchwoman's plan? Whatever feelings she articulated in her letters must have struck a responsive chord in him. The flattery with which she persistently inundated Loti probably appealed to his massive ego, and it ensured that he would be more likely to embrace her political and social banner.

Marc Hélys's narrative records the entire adventure which she and her consoeurs concocted, as well as their reactions during the experience. The book details several meetings between Loti and herself (with her friends) and reproduces the letters which she sent pretending that she was Leyla – a Leyla who was an unhappy, oppressed woman with a sad marital history. In these letters the supposed Leyla not only complains of her unliberated life, but she subtly changes the direction of her argument to address Loti, the hitherto disinterested observer, as attractive but unattainable lover. This shadowy figure, who meets Leyla and her 'cousins' on several occasions, is portrayed as being sympathetic to these women's plight, but even in the novelistic context, it is difficult to understand why Leyla should have been so attracted to him. Perhaps reasons of expediency explain the subplot; by giving Loti a more active rôle in the Leyla/Loti romance, Hélys enticed him into adopting her tale.

In addition, Hélys shows how her letters were often determined by real-life episodes, even when her epistolary version to Loti was invented. As the Frenchman always trusted his correspondent, he assumed that her letters contained a truthful account of her experiences; thus, he replicated their content in his finished novel. Leyla/Hélys was duplicitous; at one point, she was supposed to be in Smyrna, the city to which Loti's ship was sailing. Loti planned to meet her there, and letters were exchanged about Leyla's life in that vacation spot, as well as plans for a reunion between the two friends once he arrived. However, Marc Hélys had travelled to Sweden at the time, all of her letters to Loti having been forwarded to him through friends in Smyrna, for, as a self-supporting female journalist, she needed to earn money 'because my trip to Constantinople had cost me [some money] and our novel absorbed me for more than a year to the detriment of all other work. Without counting – as Neyr said laughingly – "all that we spent in stamps, in pretty blouses and in flowers!" '.[32] Thus Hélys fabricated and mingled several untruths; she told Loti that she was in a city which she had actually never visited, and compounded that lie by vividly describing the life which she led there – which information Loti then copied into one of his letters in *Les Désenchantées*.

Although Hélys' letters appeared spontaneous and her reactions very passionate, her conception of the novel Loti would write was premeditated. She knew precisely what the plot outline should be and expressed her views in the succeeding letter, a portion of which would be useful to reproduce here, both to understand the Frenchwoman's overall plan and to be able to better interpret Loti's emendations:

And here is how I imagined your book: A man wrote a book one day wherein he placed his heart alone with his memories of youth. Then the memories succeeded each other; his loves also. He became sceptical, and life spoiled him and sickened him.

One day, in France, in his Parisian life, he receives a letter written in a harem. He had almost forgotten. The letter tells him that time has passed, that the Oriental female recluse is no longer a doll. It describes another life to him. It expresses thoughts, dreams, anguish . . . He finally wants to see, to know his correspondents. He is curious about feelings. He is a dilettante.

He returns to Stamboul to search again for his youth, his impressions of freshness, his enthusiasms. He finally understands her [the one] who wrote to him.

I would not make of him one of these fatal beings who sows unhappiness and goes away. I would only create him into an artist, a dilettante, impassioned by new and exquisite impressions.

And what can happen to him if not love? But love of her; not of him. He is only an artist; he loves life [to be] beautiful and neat. This adventure charms him because it reveals an unknown world to him. He would voluntarily go to the end of the adventure; but this would be for him only an adventure.

Whether or not a Turkish woman proceeds to the end of her love, the end of the story is flight or death. But our hero cannot disturb his life: he is married. And my heroine is too proud to go away with him and be only his mistress.

She dies thus; not because of this man, but suffocated by her dreams, broken by the fetters which lock her up and leave her with no means of *consoling herself for this love by action*. [Hélys's emphasis]

One part of your novel will be in letters; the remainder in diary fragments. The empty spots, the side which pertains to Moslem life, we would send to you. You would need only to rewrite it. We would make a family live for you. All of it would be true except for exterior details. And thus you would have the intimate life of the Orient as recounted by Oriental women.[33]

Loti's novel is longer and more fleshed out than Hélys's work. *Les Désenchantées* contains about 82,000 words; *Le Secret des Désenchantées* about 52,000. When one considers that a good part of the latter includes an itemisation of various rendezvous between the four protagonists (some of which are not mentioned in the fiction) as well as a lengthy justification for Hélys's project and her motives, one can see that Loti necessarily elaborated her work. Of the 24 letters she claims she received from her correspondent[34] she reproduces 19 in her text and shows how Loti used them in his. Sometimes he converted letters into dialogue,[35] sometimes he took part of a letter or extracted a single description;[36] sometimes two or more letters were blended into a single one.[37] On occasion, the entire letter was reproduced, virtually unchanged.[38]

Nevertheless, Loti retained the basic plot outline, making only a few minor changes. The 'elderly' writer preferred the Bay of Biscay to Paris, and he was transposed into a bachelor whose attraction for Djénane is clear. Hélys's letters to Loti imply that Leyla's desirability emanated from her personality and her personal magnetism. Loti insisted that Djénane's eyes were green, reminiscent of Aziyadé's, and that her allure consisted as much in her resemblance to his past love as it did in the emotions elicited by the present one.

Not only did Loti alter the original emphasis in Hélys's letters, but he expanded upon her treatment of death ·and his former mistress's memory. *Les Désenchantées* is sprinkled with various descriptions of trips to the cemetery where Nedjibé's spirit is lovingly kept alive. Marc Hélys and her friends consciously kept the thought of Loti's past love before him by suggesting and then implementing visits to the grave, but Loti's fictional account was designed so as to place even the initial contact between the Turkish women and himself in a life/love/death relationship, thus causing the reader to relate the past and the present, life and death, with the women.[39] Loti's obsession with death (as explored above in previous chapters) is once again pursued here.

The emphasis on death is far more marked in the Loti version than in Hélys's text. The spectre of the dead Nedjibé haunts the entire book and serves as a touchstone for evoking fond memories of a woman loved. It is the cemetery which recalls happy memories, and it is a living woman who evokes the dead girl, whom Loti had chosen to love and leave. The commingling of love and death is more pronounced in this text than in any previous one.

Besides the heightened emphasis on death, the French novel contains many passages of description of Stamboul at various times of the year and in different guises, along with detailed accounts of Ottoman home life and Turkish customs.[40] Loti was far more interested in portraying Turkish society and the physical locale than was his French compatriot. Hélys focused almost exclusively on her heroine and her reactions to her unhappy situation. For Hélys, Loti as character becomes important only inasmuch as he provides an outlet for her heroine's emotions. For Loti, the 'veiled shadows' provide the excuse to teach his hero about one aspect of Turkish life and culture – the plight of the Turkish woman in one small segment of society. Finally, Loti includes more material on Mélek and Zeyneb than does his woman friend, whose letters to the Frenchman were mainly signed by Leyla. Both Hélys and Loti, however, present their heroines as disillusioned because their intellectual and cultural aspirations remain unfulfilled.

Even though André Lhéry is exposed to three 'disenchanted' women, the Oriental appeal of Stamboul[41] (and Stamboul is paradigmatic for Turkey) is too great for him to be disillusioned with this non-Occidental civilisation.

> But at this hour, he loved all this Stamboul passionately, whose thousands of evening lights began to be reflected in the sea; something attached him there desperately, he didn't define it well, something which floated in the air above the immense and diverse city, doubtless an emanation of feminine souls, – because in the end, it is almost always that which attaches us to places or objects – the feminine souls which he had loved and which mingled together.[42]

It is interesting to note that Stamboul – probably Loti's only real love – is equated here with 'feminine souls' and that it is these ethereal 'emanations' which ultimately account for an attachment to places or objects.

In the Loti text, Lhéry, the jaded author, becomes more sympathetic because he is depicted less passively than his real-life counterpart in Hélys's non-fictional account. Another change from Hélys's version is Loti's description of André Lhéry and his importance to the harem women.[43] He is portrayed so attractively that all three women appear enamoured of him, although it is Djénane, the most attractive of the three, who is most affected. Hélys's version features Djénane's involvement only.

It is not enough for Loti to stress his hero's appeal merely to the heroines of *Les Désenchantées*; according to his novel, women, generically, respond positively to his fictional *alter ego*.[44] The novel begins with the author, Lhéry, poring over letters from his many admirers, 'letters from women, for the most part, some signed, others are not, carrying to the writer the incense of pretty intellectual adorations'.[45] Although he felt a responsibility to answer his fans, he usually found himself too busy 'and the poor letters accumulated, to be drowned soon after under the flood of the following ones and to end up in oblivion'.[46]

Loti cannot restrain himself from endowing his hero with such universal appeal that all women (and the 'fantômes noirs' are just three representatives of the entire gender) are infatuated by his charm, and the reader is made very aware that the number of his admirers is legion. At one point, Lhéry chides Djénane for not wanting to see him again 'because you made me a pleasing declaration of intellectual friendship! What childishness! I receive many others like it, and they don't affect me at all'.[47] What is surprising about his relationship with the three 'disenchanted' women, who are 'disenchanted' because their aspirations can never be reconciled with their reality,[48] is not that they should be attracted to him (for this is a *conditio sine qua non*), but given his egoistic bent, that he would be affected by them.[49]

Furthermore, all Loti's past affiliations with Oriental women were explicitly sexual and presumably satisfying to him. Lhéry's relationship with Djénane, alone in the entire Loti canon, is not actually sexual, and yet the tenor of the association is more highly charged, more implicitly amorous, than any of the previous carnal ones. What can we deduce from this? One obvious conclusion is that Loti was not as comfortable with a heterosexual physical relationship as he purported to be. As a result, a non-physical, intellectual and emotional liaison was more desirable for him. Further, the lack of bodily contact in every sense – the veiled beings who rarely reveal their facial features, the epistolary friendship which requires no bodily contact at all, the constant presence of a group of women (never less than two and usually at least three) – ensured that Lhéry/Loti was safe from sexual touch.

The fear of any permanent association is so great that Loti has all three heroines die: two from physical ailments and one from suicide, but all three deaths are expressions of revolt against the exigencies of marriage. Mélek dies passively of brain fever, clearly caused by 'nervous overexcitement', 'revolt', and 'terror'[50] occasioned by her forthcoming marriage. For Zeyneb, her 'délivrance' lies in her chest infection, which she refuses to treat – a means of avoiding wedlock. Djénane's suicide is prompted by her enforced remarriage to Hamdi Bey. This incident alone was suggested by Hélys; the others are imaginative embellishments on the original.

It is marriage, then, which causes the women to revolt, for marriage is the symbol of oppression, of that which is negative in the lives of these cultured, attractive, well-educated 'Turkish' females. What is curious here is that Loti should have initiated such a profound change over Hélys's version, since so much of her text was followed, and almost verbatim at that. By causing all the women to expire, Loti not only tries to impose a stronger statement on his audience, but he succeeds in repeating the phallocentric formula which invests all his works – the male fantasy that wishes to dismiss all women with which it comes into contact by eliminating them. We might even go further to infer that these relationships with women have been fictionally transmuted to reach their inevitable conclusion – termination. Although the hero appears genuinely to lament his loss after each experience, the pattern is so repetitive that one can only question the nature of the grief felt each time.

> Surely one of the central questions that such love stories raise is why their emotional charge so often depends on the death of the woman and so rarely on the death of the man. Why the death of a beautiful woman, as Poe suggested, should be such an unfailing source of 'universal' melancholy is a question well worth pondering. Certainly one of its implications is that the tears are a luxury enjoyed by the survivor who is male and male-identified, and that at some level the experience is factitious and dishonest.[51]

Thus we see that even in Loti's most feminist work, one whose basic outlines and initial experiences were contrtibuted by a woman and whose theme is sympathetic to women, what must be the French novelist's deep-seated gender distinctions serve to undermine an otherwise pro-feminine position.

Although the initial intent of the novel was to polemicise and proselytise on behalf of modern Turkish women, this goal was less successfully achieved than it would have been had the unnecessary sub-plot involving Lhéry and Djénane been omitted. Djénane's dissatisfaction with her current situation did not require a love displacement toward André Lhéry. By deflecting her unhappiness away from her real problem (her divorced situation in a country which did not sanction unmarried women) and investing her with unexpressed love for the elderly writer, the reader is confused by a double message – is she committing suicide as a political statement against the oppression of Turkish women, or is she taking her life in a romantic gesture of *Weltschmerz* because she can never hope to marry the European with whom she has inexplicably fallen in love? And if it is for the latter reason, why is there so little preparation given for this motive in the text? One possible reading for the ending is that Djénane's death represented Loti's feelings about the conflict between Western and Oriental civilisations – he felt that the Ottoman life he knew and loved was slowly dying under the incursion of Western civilisation, and he mourned its demise even as he recognised its inevitability. Lhéry's departure from Stamboul is surrounded with the prospect of death 'not only for each of us who will have to die, but for those after who will see the last of our generation fall, Islam come to an end, and our declining races disappear'.[52]

The theme of the corrosive effect of European civilisation on primitive, innocent societies is reiterated by Zeyneb at the end of *Les Désenchantées*. When she discovers Djénane's death, she writes a bitter letter to Loti blaming her friend's death on the Occidental ideas and influence to which she had been exposed.

> And she would have lived, had she remained the little barbarian, the little princess of the Asian plains! She would never have known about the nothingness of things. It is thinking too much and knowing too much which poisoned her, each day a little more. It is the Occident which killed her, André. If one had left her primitive and ignorant, only beautiful, I would [still] see her there near me, and I would [still] hear her voice.[53]

Here Loti subscribes to the simplistic notion that primitive, simple, 'unspoiled' life is preferable to the more sophisticated and enlightened life-style characteristic of Western culture. But Djénane never was a 'little barbarian', for she had been raised (as Loti took pains to inform his readers) in a privileged, European-inspired environment of which she was justly proud. Her personal situation (Hamdi Bey's deception and adultery) were as much the causes of her discontent as her inability to find expression for her intellectual and emotional needs. Personal frustration and the inability to convert her aspirations and knowledge into constructive activity led to her demise rather than 'the Occident'.

Despite the leitmotiv of death and unfulfilled desire in this novel, *Les Désenchantées* is the one work in which Loti had no need for self-recrimination during this real-life adventure and its fictional account, as he was not the instrument of his heroine's downfall. Previously, the more he plunged into voluptuousness, the more he was bored with its aftermath.[54] Now the exotic was erotic precisely because it was unattainable. Richards maintains that 'it was a love, unexpressed throughout a good portion of the account, but coming forth with profusion at the end, when it was too late'[55]; I disagree with this assessment. Neither character openly expresses affection for the other prior to the last letter, but many instances occur throughout the novel when the various characters allude to strong feelings for one another: 'Because you, too, André, you will not forget me any more.' 'The days which passed, without another summons from these unknown women, made the idea that he would never again hear Zahidé's strangely gentle voice from under her veil, almost painful.' 'Oh, André! In souls whose passions have been curbed for a long time like ours, if you knew what an ideal feeling composed of admiration and tenderness is.'[56] These sentiments, however, are based on fantasy rather than reality. Djénane knows little about Lhéry, as their conversations deal primarily with the women and their lives and touch on the author's life only when they discuss Nedjibé, his former love. Thus, when Djénane writes her famous letter of farewell elevating André, the confidant, to André, the lover, she not only writes to a man she does not know well, but she addresses a passive rather than an active Occidental lover – a new rôle for the Loti hero.

Not only did Loti describe a different type of love relationship in *Les Désenchantées* than he had heretofore, but he experienced a profound emotional attachment to Leyla/Marc Hélys, which he immediately translated into print. Unlike the other novels which were written retrospectively, this last fictional work was produced directly after the event, so Loti's sensibilities were more immediately involved. In addition, the presence of the letters served as a constant reminder of the recent drama in which he had participated,[57] and he truly felt that he was a privileged Westerner whose duty it was to disseminate the information which he, alone as a male, possessed.

By and large, however, Loti's emotional thrust paralleled that of Hélys, and the recurring themes mentioned in the previous Oriental novels take on a different tone. The preoccupation with death and its association with love is certainly evident here, but the Frenchman is kinder to his feminine friends than he is in any previous Oriental text. Unlike the other works in which he effectively overcomes a language barrier, in this novel Loti requires only French to speak with his 'phantoms'. Furthermore, the animal imagery is virtually non-existent. Nor is this the only way in which he communicates differently; he now functions as a passive observer. He is little more than a receptacle for their sentiments and outpourings, giving little of himself to them. In previous works, Loti's most effective communication with women was sexual; here the lack of physical contact intensifies rather than defuses the relationship.

Notwithstanding these changes, instances of self-aggrandisement and ego inflation still occur to remind the reader that the author has not totally abandoned his old style. As in so much of the 'Oriental' oeuvre, Loti, the hero, is accompanied by a male companion who witnesses his successes with women. In *Les Désenchantées*, as in his previous works, Loti shares his intimate thoughts with his Occidental sailor friend rather than with the Oriental women, probably because his new-found friends, despite their educational advantages, could not be expected to understand the finer elements of the male soul.

Nor would a total turnabout be realistic for a 56-year-old famous novelist who had attained renown by appealing to European tastes. Hence his long-held conventional beliefs in male supremacy still obtained. Even as he appears to admire the three modern young women, his previous posture intrudes into his writing to prevent him from being totally complimentary toward them. Marc Hélys, of course, never made these distinctions in her characterisations. For example, when Loti first describes Djénane, Mélek, and Zeyneb, he compares their mental aptitude with that of their 'somnolent' forebears who did not have the advantages of modern education: 'In their [the young girls'] brain, composed of new or long-sleeping matter, everything germinated miraculously, as in virgin territory, the long, rank weeds and the pretty, poisonous flowers.'[58]

This condescending attitude toward women is mouthed not only by the narrator, but by the heroines themselves. Both Zeyneb and Djénane make disparaging comments about their intellects or the effects of Western thinking upon them. ' "So there," said Djénane while laughing, "this is how we are. As soon as one scratches the veneer a bit [one finds] little barbarians." '[59] Zeyneb is particularly self-deprecatory; despite her Western education and enlightened views, she cannot accept feminine independence. She implores Loti to befriend the three women, for they need a man, 'someone with whom these poor, forgotten, humiliated creatures could speak, exchange their little views, most often fearful and innocent'.[60]

Loti, the narrator, tries to counteract these negative impressions of his 'fantômes' by creating an atmosphere of learning and literary exposure for them. In Chapter 2, he first describes his youthful heroine. He emphasises her eclecticism by representing the hallmarks of a superior Western education in Djénane's bedroom (letters in disarray over the table, notations on paper indicating musical composition 'as in a fever of composition',[61] books by the Countess of Noailles, Verlaine, Kant, and Nietzsche). The general effect is certainly impressive; subsequent comments about the heroine's linguistic facility reinforces this impression. Particularly noteworthy is her admiration for the great French author, André Lhéry. Nevertheless, Loti's former attitudes toward the Oriental woman reappear: despite Djénane's obvious intellectual and artistic achievements, she lacks discernment. 'Doubtless no *mother* [author's emphasis] was in this house who would supervise the readings and moderate the overheating of this young brain.'[62] On the other hand, Loti gives credit to the *mother* rather than the father, to show the discrimination necessary to guide her youngster through the thickets of knowledge.

Once Djénane does try to impress Lhéry with her originality by suggesting to him a plot for his new book, Loti, the narrator, says: 'He understood then, that just then he caused her suffering [when he] opposed with semi-mockery her little literary ideas, which she had come to by herself, with so much effort, and sometimes with a marvellous intuition.'[63] Loti acknowledges his heroine's sensitivity, and gives her credit for her 'intuition' at the same time as he depreciates her ideas. The emphasis on 'little literary ideas', on the enormous 'effort' to achieve insight and the 'marvellous intuition', disparage the intellectual achievement. By discounting intuition and implying elevated ratiocination alone as an acceptable avenue to knowledge, he undermines Djénane's very worthwhile suggestions.

This ambivalence recurs throughout the novel. Loti wants to credit his heroines with rationality and perceptive powers, but his need for superiority, his long-held convictions, continually articulated throughout the 'Oriental' oeuvre – that these women were passive, dependent, primitive, and simple (intellectually as well as emotionally) – constantly interfere with his more equitable vision. Thus, for every generous statement ('And today, conversing with an Occidental man, and a man of renown, they found themselves on the same level; and he, in treating them as equals, as intelligent beings, as *souls*, brought to them a kind of intoxication of the mind heretofore unfelt'[64]) one encounters its opposite. Even when he tries to be magnanimous, he adopts a condescending tone, one of visible superiority ('he . . . brought to them a kind of intoxication of the mind') which implies that he was the source of their new-found enlightenment. Thus, when he speaks of the girls' elderly tutors, the women who trained their students to read and think in Western terms, he states: 'It appeared to André that they were at the same time high-minded and naïve, these two semi-old women; for the rest, distinguished and extremely well-educated, but with a romantic exaltation a bit old-fashioned in 1904.'[65] Here again, it is difficult for the author to give full credit to feminine intellectual accomplishment. Although these women are clearly responsible for their protégées' achievements, Loti cannot restrain himself from some negative qualifiers: 'semi-old', 'naïve', and possessing 'romantic exaltation a bit old-fashioned in 1904'.

Nevertheless, one can find a new tone in this work – that of a man willing to acknowledge feminine intellectual ability – and this was due to the profound influence Hélys exerted upon him, both personally and as a representative of the modern Oriental woman. It may be that his favourable treatment of the 'new' Turkish woman was a means of redressing the wrongs he felt he had committed toward Aziyadé. He felt himself responsible for her death, and *Les Désenchantées* may have been a form of 'blood money' for him.[66] In any event, there is no question that the reader is left with a far more favourable impression of women (albeit from a very select class) at the end of this novel than after reading any of Loti's previous 'Oriental' fiction.

Despite Loti's more positive image of the Turkish woman as a thinking being in *Les Désenchantées* as opposed to previous works, and despite his stridently evangelical tone, the social/political side of this novel was nonetheless based on inaccurate information and false perceptions, which Marc Hélys freely admitted in her work – though of course, never to Loti himself. Loti never bothered to investigate whether the plight of the Turkish woman was in actuality as his correspondent indicated. As a result, he disseminated an image of Western-influenced women who were totally oppressed by their condition as females in a male-oriented society. Despite their educational advantages (private tutors, musical and artistic guidance), financial security, and Occidental exposure, the women were unable to interact with men, except in a very restricted manner. By and large, they were shielded from outsiders through the institution of the harem, and they were permitted to speak only to their spouses and male members of their family. They were considered odalisks[67] with no other function than to please the men whom they married. These weddings were usually arranged, and it was unthinkable for a woman to be unmarried or to seek a career, whether or not she were wed.

Loti's highly romanticised view of the life of the Ottoman woman, even the upper class one, does not conform to the reality that prevailed. In Chapter 3, I explored briefly the actual position of women in the Ottoman Empire, and it is clear that Loti's impression is, at best, only partially correct. The women in *Les Désenchantées* are portrayed as 'frivolous' and 'foolishly sentimental' but, in general, upper-class Ottoman women of the late nineteenth century were socially and politically aware. In a sensible and practical manner, they were working for reforms that would enhance their position, seeking above all, to strengthen their opportunities for modern education.[68] Until then (1904), they were essentially restricted to a traditional religious education and, although many of them were well-educated, the importance of further exposure to modern knowledge was apparent to them.

Closely related to the inaccurate impression of the education of these women is the way the French author describes their cultural orientation; according to Loti, they were quite Western-oriented and regarded European culture as the ideal. There is evidence, however, that many Ottoman women resented rather than desired Occidental influence as they did not perceive it to be attractive or beneficial. Demetra Vaka, for example, recounts a visit to a Turkish harem of the same class as Hélys described, and her conversations with her Turkish friends there confirm this Oriental attitude. 'Musselmen women, with the help of Mahomet, ought to work out their own salvation, and borrow nothing from the West. We are a race apart, with different traditions and associations.'[69] Their political-social position stemmed from local roots and seems to have been self-imposed rather than Occident-inspired.[70]

Clearly, the portrayal of these women as idle pleasure-seekers is not valid. Though this stereotypical view was widespread, it had little basis in fact, as has been pointed out by a noted Turkish female author of the period who has written:

The laziness attributed to Turkish women in the West is applicable to a much smaller minority in Turkey than elsewhere. They have at all times been hard workers. Both in the fields and in their homes, and in the earlier arts and crafts, Turkish women have always been much more hard-working, responsible, and well-balanced beings than men.[71]

The degree to which women were dependent on men has also been exaggerated. Women were not as highly supervised and guarded as is suggested by Loti's work. Even harem women enjoyed a much freer existence. They were never kept behind bars; grilles, where these existed, usually on the ground floor of houses, were designed to keep thieves out. Women in general were not prohibited from leaving their homes after sundown; on the contrary, they visited each other more at this time than men did.[72]

One should not be surprised, therefore, that two Turkish critics intuited that the three characters in *Les Désenchantées* were actually European rather than Turkish. 'We take them rather for three Frenchwomen disguised as Turkish women!'[73] How poorly Loti had portrayed the reality of the Ottoman woman is suggested by the conclusion reached independently by another Ottoman intellectual. Sefer Bey wrote: 'No, M. Lhéry, the woman who wrote to you is not the Moslem of year 1332. She can be the product of a very brilliant imagination . . . she can be French, English, German, or American, but never Turkish!'[74]

Hence one must accept the insightful conclusion reached by a Western woman who knew the Ottoman scene well. She wrote:

> Pierre Loti's novel, *Les Désenchantées*, has unfortunately been taken by the majority of the numerous readers of that in many respects delightful book as a typical picture of the life of the educated Osmanli woman of today. By all who possess an adequate knowledge of Eastern life this work is, however, condemned as presenting an entirely false view of the aspirations and ideals of representative Osmanli womanhood.[75]

Les Désenchantées, then, is something of a curiosity. As a sociological document (which it purports to be) and polemic on the plight of the Turkish woman, it is persuasive but inaccurate. The reader is certainly moved by the situation of the women as designated in the text, but that predicament is grossly exaggerated and unrealistic. As fiction, the work leaves something to be desired. Although the character of Djénane is well-developed, all the other 'Turkish' characters are marginal to the text. André Lhéry's character is too passive to be interesting; he symbolises the Western observer who is fascinated by a culture which is both alien and attractive to him. The book is as much a nostalgic return to a once-beloved foreign culture which contained fond memories for the hero (one of the chief appeals these women held for him was their reminder of his earlier, youthful love) as it is a bittersweet acknowledgement of the ageing process and the ever-present spectre of death. Just as Marc Hélys duped Loti with her highly romanticised but not unbelievable tale, so Loti, in turn, deceived his many readers into believing what Edward Said would term another 'Orientalist' fiction. Unfortunately, the document served to reinforce Occidental preconceptions about Turkey rather than provide an accurate introduction to Ottoman life.

One question still needs to be examined. Why did Marc Hélys give Pierre Loti all the necessary information to write *Les Désenchantées* instead of authoring the book herself? She gives us the answer in her own words: 'But I knew that what I could write myself would not carry as much weight with the public as would a book of Pierre Loti's.'[76] In addition, she was proud of her association with the renowned French author, and took pleasure in her clandestine activity. 'I obeyed a very natural feeling of pride and joy to have collaborated, unknown, in a very beautiful work.'[77] She anticipates questions which enquire why she revealed her secret publicly, and she answers them by praising Loti's invention and his ability to accept a novel and interpret it poetically – with the clear implication that his inspiration would be more successful than hers.[78]

Although she gives Loti due credit for his poetic powers, her confession was certainly written to set the record straight, and was designed to let the world know that this romance was as much her achievement as Loti's. And this, then, finally explains the singular position of *Les Désenchantées* in the Frenchman's oeuvre and why it is so feminist in orientation. The reason this last novel is so different from all the 'Oriental' novels which preceded it is that it was essentially conceived and written by a woman.

7

Conclusion

Pierre Loti's greatest literary strength lay in his vivid impressionistic renderings of places and events based on his actual experiences. He was not a voracious reader; on the contrary, he created something of a literary scandal during his acceptance speech for the Académie française by announcing proudly, 'I never read.'[1] If he had been more knowledgeable about the societies which he visited and wrote about, he would have provided a much richer context for his novels, though it is not likely, given his orientation, that he would have portrayed women in any less stereotypical fashion.

From a literary perspective, what distinguishes this novelist from so many others is that his works are endowed with semi-documentary qualities – Loti probably recorded what he saw (to this day he remains one of the truly great 'évocateurs' of exotic locales) – which suggest to the reader that his representations of the culture and society are accurate. As Loti's prior knowledge of the countries he visited was sparse and his interests limited to the visual (that is, he seems to be concerned exclusively with his impressions and what he saw), he never developed more than a superficial knowledge of the culture. This means that his writing provides a record of events with no explication of cultural values and structures. Hence, those Westerners who read his works under the impression that he is offering an accurate representation of the society being depicted, labour under a misapprehension. In reality, he perpetuates some of the cultural clichés of the time.

This is particularly true of his attitude toward Oriental women. The attributes with which he invests these feminine characters reflect more closely his private and psychological needs than they do the actual position of women in their societies. For the most part, they are portrayed as objects for his delectation – simple, primitive, dependent instruments existing exclusively for his sexual satisfaction.

The particular women he describes are clearly exemplars of his Occidental vision of the generic species of the land; Rarahu,

117

Aziyadé, and Fatou-gaye are supposedly representative of Tahitian, Turkish, or Senegalese women. Hence, even though these, like all his other feminine characters derive from a simplistic vision – regardless of cultural variations, they are all remarkably similar and they all possess identical attitudes toward men – foreigners reading his works can legitimately infer that women in the various countries he visited are, by and large, like those he describes.

Since all the Oriental women essentially support and ratify their Occidental lovers, it is proper to conclude that Loti created these fictional characters as wish-fulfilment fantasies, to simultaneously reinforce and magnify his manhood. Although the nominal centre of attention in all his fiction is a female, almost every novel discussed finds one or more males lurking importantly in the background. Loti's relationships with these men are questionable; thus it is reasonable to assume that the feminine focus acts as a screen for possible homosexual activity, or minimally, as a diversion from less acceptable forms of social interaction.

With all the subterfuge which the author provides in dealing with his male friends (both Occidental and Oriental), on one point he is absolutely clear – the Occidental men are always his intellectual companions and his trusted confidants. Oriental women provide diversion from ennui; they fulfil his and his *alter ego*'s physical requirements, and they supply necessary companionship against loneliness and the fear of death – an ever-present obsession for him. Intellectually, however, they are regarded as inferior. Their world is circumscribed by essentially frivolous undertakings; all the women lead fundamentally hedonistic existences – none is shown to be hard-working or struggling to survive. All have servants or live carefree lives that imply no need for industriousness. In this fantasy land, poverty is unknown and happiness dependent on momentary gratification.

Thus, Loti, the hero, or his protagonist are always fully in command of any and every situation. They are never disappointed in love[2] nor do they suffer any personal setbacks. The Occidentals are the objects of fawning devotion and great admiration by all the Oriental women – who serve as vehicles for masculine aggrandisement. Their rôle, in short, is to enhance the position of the male.

Loti's fictive vision of women conformed to nineteenth-century sexist attitudes. Although he socialised with a number of well-known, accomplished, and successful women throughout his life, he did not pattern his feminine characters on them. He wanted no competition in his imaginative production from anyone who would detract from his or his protagonist's importance. Only in his final novel does he portray women who have some of the qualities of his women friends, and this, as noted earlier, was due to a woman's influence.

Although Loti was always receptive to new sensations and experiences, he was not as tolerant of new ideas. By and large he wanted to keep women in their place – meaning both as subservient to men and in their cultural settings as he knew them. Thus, he opposed any kind of progress and wanted to maintain conditions in all the countries he visited as they were or, preferably, to turn the clock back to a more traditional state. This colonialist mentality also reflects prevailing contemporary nineteenth-century attitudes.

He considered himself as something of an authority on the several countries he knew and lived in for some time, and particularly on their women. He was asked to participate in a conference on 'Feminine Life' in March 1914, where he consented to speak on 'La Femme turque' ('The Turkish Woman') before a large gathering of European ladies.[3] This speech aptly summarises Loti's views on women. The importance of the talk is twofold: it crystalises many of Loti's views on Oriental women, and it provides further evidence of his use of women. As Loti's last public statement on Oriental women, this speech encapsulates all the Occidental stereotypes on which he had been nurtured.

He began by comparing Oriental women favourably to their Western counterparts, at least in matters of dress and style. The discreet, fully covered 'tcharchafs' with their complementary veils would form a harmonious grouping in contrast to the Occidental image before him, which reminded him of 'a meeting of Redskins who had just adorned themselves in preparation for a scalp-dance!'.[4] Why the comparison? The seated ladies were all wearing hats with feathers and the self-styled early environmentalist speaker chastised the group for its disregard for the varied species which provided their modishness. On this occasion, Loti marginalised the entire female sex by mocking their fashions, thus undermining their judgement; he could not understand why 'the dream of some of them [the Turkish ladies], already a bit unbalanced by your example, would be, alas! to dare to wear hats as you do'.[5] Here Occidental as well as Oriental women are disparaged; the former provides a poor model which the latter is too 'unbalanced' to judge properly.

Although nominally approving the entry of emancipated Turkish women into careers or professions, Loti subverts this endorsement by citing cases of 'modern' women who renounced their progressive ideas at the end of their lives[6] or adulterous women who attempted to murder family members as retaliation against family injustice.[7]

The anecdotes he relates are interesting but pointless; there is no focus to the speech and he gives lip service to progress and co-operation between the Frenchwomen and their Turkish sisters ('Help them and reach out for them, but tell them not to run too quickly along unknown paths leading to the future')[8] while ending his lecture with his reiterated message: 'Open the cages, open all the harems. Yet don't open them too quickly, for fear that the young, imprisoned birds should take a frantic flight before knowing properly where their inexperienced and fragile wings will take them.'[9]

Whether in fiction or in actuality, Loti can only see women in terms of small, defenceless creatures. The young imprisoned birds with fragile wings must be slowly guided by their more experienced sisters; his conservative mentality precludes the thought that Oriental women shake off the masculine fetters which bind them to their traditional rôles, or that they seek male models with which to express their new-found freedom. As French female rôle models were relatively passive,[10] Loti felt comfortable in citing them as examplars for the Turkish women, on whom he considered himself an authority.

Once again the French author injects his own perceptions and opinions into what was to have been an objective assessment of 'The Turkish Woman'. Although he acknowledges that Turkish women have increased access to the professions and to jobs while praising them for their quick-wittedness and eminent educability, he concedes that they are 'rather too educated for my taste'[11] and admits that they retain their Oriental spirit under a 'veneer of modernism'[12] which suits Loti very well. As long as progress is contained within very narrow boundaries, as long as the new is able to coexist with the old, Loti is willing to permit development to take place. But when the new must supplant the old – then Loti urges caution, because he ultimately does not trust women to have sufficient sagaciousness to be able to choose a wise course of action without his experienced guidance. In exhorting his Occidental sisters to help their Oriental consoeurs, Loti is once again insisting upon his rôle as superior and implying that without his assistance, all women (but particularly Oriental women) would be at a serious disadvantage.

Although this speech was given in 1914, it expresses nineteenth-century views. Just as his prescriptions for feminine equality are difficult for modern women to accept, his views toward Oriental women are quaint – decidedly products of his time. Yet Loti was not a man who could be stereotyped easily. He remained an individualist, who was profoundly influenced by the cultural prejudices of his age while simultaneously espousing unorthodox views in his private and public life. He longed for the traditional but was willing to accept ideas which were not consonant with his previous positions. He certainly deserves credit for his willingness to accept Marc Hélys's arguments dealing with the need for reform in the position of Turkish women. Even though the information which he received from her and her friends was misleading, his willingness to proselytise actively on behalf of a feminist cause is impressive. Equally noteworthy is his ability to modify presumably entrenched attitudes after so many years. One of Loti's positive contributions to French literature was that he articulated, toward the end of his life, a sympathetic attitude toward Oriental women, an outlook that was quite unusual in France at that time.

Notes

NOTES TO CHAPTER 1: LITERARY OVERVIEW

1. In March 1982 I went to Paris and spent several days in the library at the Sorbonne. Near the university I went into half a dozen bookstores in order to buy some of Loti's works. His name was unknown in several of them, and I found only one copy of *Pêcheur d'Islande* in a 'livre de poche'.

2. See the Introduction to Simone de Beauvoir, *The Second Sex*, trs. H. M. Parshley (New York: Alfred A. Knopf, 1953).

3. Susan Gubar, ' "The Blank Page" and the Issues of Female Creativity', in *Writing and Sexual Difference*, ed. Elizabeth Abel (Chicago: University of Chicago Press, 1982) p. 73.

4. Sylvia G. Haim, 'The Arab Woman in the Mirror of Literature', *Middle East Studies*, 17, no. 4 (October 1981) p. 518: 'Whatever his rôle the Algerian man . . . tries to make an object of woman [chosifier la femme].'

5. Luce Irigaray, 'Ce sexe qui n'en est pas un', in *New French Feminisms: An Anthology*, eds Elaine Marks and Isabelle de Courtivron (Amherst, Mass.: University of Massachusetts Press, 1980) p. 105.

6. H. R. Hays, *The Dangerous Sex: The Myth of Feminine Evil* (New York: G. P. Putnam's Sons, 1964) p. 282.

7. Betty S. Flowers, 'The "I" in Adrienne Rich: Individuation and the Androgyne Archetype', in *Theory and Practice of Feminist Literary Criticism*, eds Gabriela Mora and Karen S. Hooft (Ypsilanti, Mich.: Bilingual Press, 1982) p. 17.

8. de Beauvoir, *The Second Sex*, p. xxv.

9. Kate Millett, *Sexual Politics* (New York: Doubleday, 1970).

10. Elaine Showalter, *A Literature of their Own: British Women Novelists from Brontë to Lessing* (Princeton, N.J.: Princeton University Press, 1977), and Sandra M. Gilbert and Susan Gubar in *The Madwoman in the Attic: The Woman Writer and the Nineteenth-Century Literary Imagination* (New Haven, Conn.: Yale University Press, 1979) discuss the secondary role relegated to women in nineteenth-century British literature and the difficulty of a woman artist writing because of her problems with her female identity and artistic self-definition. These difficulties originate, of course, in the societal expectations of women at that time.

11. Cathérine Clément and Hélène Cixous in *La Jeune née* (Paris: Union Générale d'Editions, 1975) as well as in their many articles and books represent the newest and most advanced thinking among French feminists. Their 'Série Féminin Futur' which is dedicated 'to interrogate and analyze, the history of woman in the process of creating herself' culls from a variety of fields: philosophical,

theoretical, psychological, linguistic, political, sociological, and literary, in order to advance the cause of feminism.

12. Judith Fetterley, *The Resisting Reader* (Bloomington, Ind.: Indiana University Press, 1977), Judith Fryer, *The Faces of Eve: Women in the Nineteenth-Century American Novel* (New York: Oxford University Press, 1976), and Annette Kolodny in her many articles, especially 'Dancing Through the Minefield: Some Observations on the Theory, Practice, and Politics of a Feminist Literary Criticism', *Feminist Studies*, 6, no. 1 (Spring 1980), direct American literary criticism to a new understanding of the role of gender in American literature.

13. I recognise that feminist studies necessarily embrace any study of literature; this brief survey touches only upon some of my own research and readings. For an investigation into feminist readings in sociology and history, see Chapter 3.

14. See Edward Said, *Orientalism* (New York: Vintage Books, 1979).

15. See Mario Praz, *The Romantic Agony*, trs. Angus Davidson, 2nd edn (Oxford: Oxford University Press, 1970) p. 120.

16. 'It is ingenious to describe masochism and suffering as inherently feminine . . . [It] justifies any conceivable domination or humiliation forced upon the female as mere food for her nature. To carry such a notion to its logical conclusion, abuse is not only good for woman, but the very thing she craved' (Millett, *Sexual Politics*, pp. 194–5).

17. 'Loti a eu le culte du féminin. Il n'a pas seulement aimé *des* femmes, il a aimé la femme (Raymonde Lefêvre, *La Vie inquiète de Pierre Loti* (Paris: Société Française d'Editions Littéraires et Techniques, 1934) p. 152).

18. 'Les femmes n'existent que dans la mesure où elles servent à camper le personnage masculin' (Rolande Leguillon, 'Un aspect de l'amour chez Pierre Loti', *Rice University Studies*, 59, no. 3 (1973) p. 46.

19. Henry James, *Essays in London and Elsewhere* (New York: Harper, 1893) p. 169.

20. 'Il s'est fait le propagateur de légendes imbéciles derriere lesquelles je ne trouve jamais personne'; quoted in Pierre Flottes, *Le Drame intérieur de Pierre Loti* (Paris: Le Courrier Littéraire, 1937) p. 97.

21. N. Serban, *Pierre Loti: sa vie et son oeuvre* (Paris: Presses Françaises, 1924): 'Loti, si prolixe lorsqu'il nous parle de ses impressions et ses sensations ou de ses sentiments passagers, cache jalousement toutes ses grandes affections, toutes ses vraies douleurs' (p. 102).

22. Clive Wake, *The Novels of Pierre Loti* (The Hague: Mouton, 1974).

23. Michael G. Lerner, *Pierre Loti* (New York: Twayne Publishers, 1974) p. 40.

24. Thérèse Fallah-Najmeh in 'La Femme musulmane vue par Pierre Loti' (Thèse pour le doctorat de 3ᵉ cycle, Université de Paris IV, 1975) p. 6: 'En fait l'Orient de Loti n'est pas l'Orient des Orientaux, il est l'imaginaire à travers le réel.' She maintains that the Orient satisfied both Loti's needs for love ('sensations amoureuses') and his taste for the exotic ('goût exotique').

25. 'qu'il y a sur mon individu plusieurs couches différentes déposées par les circonstances anormales au milieu desquelles j'ai dû vivre, et

que le *moi* qui est tout au fond, le vrai celui-là, est un homme primitif, une espèce du sauvage préhistorique qui se montre de temps en temps et fait peur aux gens' (Pierre Loti, *Journal intime* (1878–1881), vol. I, ed. Samuel P. Loti-Viaud (Paris: Calmann-Lévy, 1925) p. 245).

26. Lesley Blanch, *Pierre Loti: The Legendary Romantic* (New York: Harcourt Brace Jovanovich, 1983) p. 10.

27. Robert Brown Johnson, 'A Reexamination and Revaluation of the Dual Nature in the Life and Work of Pierre Loti' (Dissertation, University of Wisconsin, 1949) p. 52.

28. 'les rêves qui s'attachaient à leur origine lointaine. "La côte orientale d'Afrique", "la mer des Indes", visions de soleil, de ciel bleu, tout un mirage fantasmagorique' (Serban, *Pierre Loti*, pp. 13–14).

29. 'Déjà le tourmentait le besoin non seulement de traduire ses sentiments, mais de les communiquer aux autres pour tâcher de les faire durer, pour arracher au néant le souvenir de ce qu'il avait connu, vécu, souffert' (Lefêvre, *La Vie inquiète de Pierre Loti*, p. 60).

30. Ibid., p. 161.

31. Helen Scribner, *Pierre Loti vu à travers son oeuvre* (Poitiers: Société Française d'Imprimerie, 1932) p. 189.

32. 'D'ailleurs il serait difficile d'exagérer la part d'affectivité féminine qui était en Loti: "le plus féminin des écrivains", affirme un critique' (Millward, *L'Oeuvre de Pierre Loti*, p. 321).

33. 'Tout en marquant périodiquement que l'action se passe au Sénégal, Loti étend la trame de ses impressions d'abord au Soudan tout entier, ensuite à la Nubie, à l'Afrique en général et enfin à la race noire tout entière' (Léon Fanoudh-Siefer, *Le Mythe du nègre et de l'Afrique noire dans la littérature française* (Paris: Librairie C. Klincksieck, 1968) p. 101.

34. 'Cet écrivain a regardé la terre d'Afrique, en y projetant son intériorité morbide et maladive, ses obsessions personelles paroxystiques. Pour lui, tout est triste, malsain, présageant la mort et le mauvais sort; tout y est mystérieux, bizarre, étrange, illogique et impur' (ibid., p. 109). Alec Hargreaves in *The Colonial Experience in French Fiction* (London: Macmillan, 1982) concurs with this interpretation: In an astute analysis of *Le Roman d'un spahi* he states: 'When Jean is described as being "de pure race blanche" ["of pure white race"], this phrase conveys more than the simple notion of his being of pure European stock; within the context of the novel, it also hints at qualities of moral purity deemed to be habitually present in white men but congenitally absent in Negroes' (p. 44).

35. 'Loti a certes été documenté sur certains points essentiels qui régissaient la société féminine musulmane en Turquie, mais il était incapable de pouvoir pénéter en profondeur l'âme de la femme et la réele existence qu'elle menait' (Fallah-Najmeh, 'La Femme musulmane', pp. 6–7).

36. Loti, *Journal intime (1878–1881)*, vol. II, p. 151. 'Tout ce qui touche de

près ou de loin à l'Islam m'attire, exerce sur moi un charme' (quoted in Fallah-Najmeh, 'La Femme musulmane', p. 40).

37. 'à travers la sensualité et la volupté auxquelles ses passions éveillées et les occasions nombreuses l'invitaient, Loti a conservé envers la femme une attitude qui pour être sous-entendue, inconsciente même, n'en est pas moins forte et se rattache étroitement à son enfance' (Basil Rafter, *La Femme dans l'oeuvre de Pierre Loti* (Paris: Presses Universitaires de France, 1938) p. 105).

NOTES TO CHAPTER 2: THE ROLE OF WOMEN IN LOTI'S LIFE

1. See Raymonde Lefêvre, *Le Mariage de Loti* (Paris: Société Française d'Editions Littéraires et Techniques, 1935), and *Les Désenchantées de Pierre Loti* (Paris: S. F. E. L. T. Editions Edgar Malfète, 1939) for parallel transcriptions of the original texts and their fictionalised versions.

2. He is almost never mentioned in his son's diaries, and the absence of strong father-figures in the mature writer's novels further attests to the weak influence of Théodore on his son.

3. 'Mon histoire serait simplement celle d'un enfant très choyé, très tenu, très obéissant ... auquel rien n'arrivait, dans son étroite sphère ouatée, qui ne fut prévu, et qu'aucun coup n'atteignait qui ne fut amorti avec une sollicitude tendre' (Pierre Loti, *Le Roman d'un enfant* (Paris: Calmann-Lévy, n.d.) pp. 1–2).

4. 'On m'a conté plus tard qu'étant tout petit, je ne laissais jamais sortir de la maison aucune personne de la famille, même pour la moindre course ou visite, sans m'être assuré que son intention était bien de revenir. "Tu reviendras, dis?" était une question que j'avais coutume de poser anxieusement après avoir suivi jusqu'à la porte ceux qui s'en allaient' (ibid., p. 3).

5. 'ma mère qui est toujours ce que j'ai de plus précieux et de plus stable, qui est toujours celle contre qui je me serre avec un reste de confiance tendre de petit enfant, quand la terreur me prend, plus sombre, de la destruction et du vide' (Pierre Loti, *Le Livre de la pitié et de la mort* (Paris: Calmann-Lévy, n.d.) p. 194).

6. Years later, Lucette married a merchant who took her to Guiana with him. There she contracted a tropical disease and returned to her home town long enough for Julien to greet her at the train station, and to be shocked by her death-like appearance. The following day, she died. Loti describes the event touchingly in *Prime Jeunesse* (Paris: Calmann-Lévy, 1919) pp. 87–91. This was the second instance in Loti's young life where he was deeply affected by a close friend or relative coming to grief as a result of exposure to exotic countries. (The news of Gustave's death had arrived in France only two months earlier.)

7. Pierre Loti, 'Vacances de Pâques', *Figures et choses qui passaient* (Paris: Calmann-Lévy, 1898).

8. Clive Wake in *The Novels of Pierre Loti* chronicles the various relationships and their importance to Loti.

9. 'Mon frère, . . . toujours mon conseiller intime et secret' (Loti, *Prime Jeunesse*, p. 53).

10. Wake, *The Novels of Pierre Loti*, p. 16.

11. Ibid., p. 19; G. Taboulet and J. C. Demariaux, *La Vie dramatique de Gustave Viaud* (n.p.: Edition du Scorpion, 1963) p. 269; Lerner, *Pierre Loti*, pp. 16–17; Blanch, *Pierre Loti*, pp. 26, 27.

12. 'Je les fis blanches, oh! blanches et roses . . . je les trouvai ravissantes ainsi' (Loti, *Le Roman d'un enfant*, p. 110). Julien's initial ideas of beauty were culturally determined.

13. Ibid., p. 111.

14. Ibid., pp. 91–3, 129, 167.

15. 'des impressions qui, aujourd'hui encore me sont pénibles et déprimantes pour peu que j'y concentre mon souvenir' (Loti, *Figures et choses*, pp. 27–8).

16. See Bird, *Pierre Loti*, passim.

17. 'J'avais déjà ce besoin de noter, de fixer des images fugitives, de *lutter contre la fragilité des choses et de moi-même* qui m'a fait poursuivre ainsi ce journal jusqu'à ces dernières années' (Loti, *Le Roman d'un enfant*, p. 238; my italics).

18. '*dans un lieu donné, dans un sphère déterminée*, et puis vieillir, et ce sera tout' (ibid., p. 225; my italics).

19. 'Et, après qu'on m'eut consulté et que j'eus répondu négligemment: "Je veux bien, ça m'est égal," la choses [sic] parut décidée' (ibid., p. 224).

20. 'L'idée que je pourrai connaître un temps où les mains bien aimées qui touchent journellement ces choses ne les toucheront jamais plus, m'est une épouvante horrible contre laquelle je ne me sens aucun courage . . . Cette corbeille à ouvrage de maman et ces tiroirs de chiffonière, c'est sans doute ce qui j'abandonnerai avec le plus de mélancolie et d'inquiétude, quand il faudra m'en aller de ce monde' (ibid., pp. 220–1).

21. 'L'idée chrétienne était restée longtemps flottante dans mon imagination alors même que je ne croyais plus; elle avait un charme vague et consolant. Aujourd'hui, ce prestige est absolument tombé; je ne connais rien de si vain, de si mensonger, de si inadmissible' (Pierre Loti, *Aziyadé* (Paris: Calmann-Lévy, 1879) p. 79).

22. 'Plus tard, pour mes amusements, j'en ai eu bien d'autres, moins faciles à conduire; mais, de tout temps, j'ai préféré les composer ainsi d'êtres plus jeunes que moi, plus jeunes d'esprit surtout, plus simples, ne contrôlant pas mes fantaisies et ne souriant jamais de mes enfantillages' (Loti, *Le Roman d'un enfant*, p. 182).

23. Ibid., p. 298.

24. 'très jeune, créole, nu-tête avec des boucles noires disposées autour du front d'une manière surannée; de beaux yeux limpides, ayant l'air de vouloir me parler, avec un mélange d'effarement triste et

d'enfantine candeur; peut-être pas absolument belle, mais possédant le suprême charme' (Loti, *Le Livre de la pitié et de la mort*, p. 8).

25. Loti, *Prime Jeunesse*, p. 136.
26. C'est l'apparence physique de ces femmes – cette "enveloppe charmante" dont Loti parlera plus tard comme une donnée nécessaire chez les femmes qu'on aime' (Scribner, *Pierre Loti*, p. 104).
27. Said, *Orientalism*, p. 188.
28. Wake, *The Novels of Pierre Loti*, p. 32.
29. Ibid., p. 28.
30. Pierre Loti, *Lettres à Mme Juliette Adam* (1880–1922) (Paris: Plon, Nourrit, 1924) p. 50.
31. Millward, *L'Oeuvre de Pierre Loti*, pp. 150, 151.
32. L'on connaît toutes les histoires de cet académicien qui aimant sonner aux portes et puis se sauver, qui adorait l'incognito, qui allait en visite en costume de matelot. "Nous disions de lui," écrit Léon Daudet, qu'il mettait un masque pour aller acheter un croissant' (ibid., p. 151). Quotation is from Léon Daudet, *Souvenir des milieux littéraires, politiques, artistiques et médicaux*, vol. I (Paris: 1920) p. 101.
33. His recent English biographers, in particular, reproduce letters and diary entries which allude to intimate experiences with men friends.
34. Wake, *The Novels of Pierre Loti*, p. 32.
35. 'précisément en entendant ce qu'elle [ma mère] venait de me dire: "Nous te garderons, toi!" je comprenais pour la première fois de ma vie tout le chemin déjà parcouru dans ma tête par ce projet à peine conscient de m'en aller aussi, de m'en aller même plus loin que mon frère, et plus partout, par le monde entier' (Loti, *Le Roman d'un enfant*, pp. 285–6).
36. Wake, *The Novels of Pierre Loti*, pp. 28ff.
37. Pierre Loti, *The Marriage of Loti*, trs. Wright and Eleanor Frierson (Honolulu: University Press of Hawaii, 1976) Introduction, p. xv.
38. 'la vérité n'est respecté que dans les détails, le fond de l'histoire n'est pas vrai: j'ai combiné plusieurs personnages réels, pour en faire un seul: Rarahu et cela me semble une étude assez fidèle de la jeune femme maorie' (Loti, *Journal intime (1878–1881)*, vol. I, p. 62).
39. Louis Bertholu in 'Préface' to Serban, *Pierre Loti*, p. xii.
40. Henri Borgeaud, 'Julien Viaud et son pseudonyme Pierre Loti', *Cahiers Pierre Loti* (November 1958) pp. 29–30.
41. 'Il passait de la vie simple, vie d'un collégien à peine émancipé à l'épanouissement inouï d'une nature exceptionellement voluptueuse et nerveuse; il vivait dans une sorte de recueillement frénétique et sensuel, intense accumulation de puissance virile' (Valence and Viaud-Loti, *La Famille de Pierre Loti*, p. 173).
42. 'Je ne puis résister à mes passions, et toutes les folies me sont possibles' (Wake, *The Novels of Pierre Loti*, p. 82).
43. 'au moins ne suis-je pas profondément corrompu; car je pleure ensuite, et j'ai horreur du mal' (ibid.).
44. Loti, *Lettres à Mme Juliette Adam*, pp. i, iv.
45. Mme Adam introduced him to many of the French writers with

whom she came in contact in Paris and provided a publication in which many of his works appeared in instalments.

46. Cornelia Otis Skinner, *Madame Sarah* (Boston, Mass.: Houghton Mifflin, 1967) p. 298.

47. 'Quand Pierre enlève ses vêtements, on dirait une statue grecque, dépouillant son enveloppe grossière et on l'admire. – Dans le même albâtre bronze, dur et poli, se dessinent les saillies mobiles des muscles, et les lignes puissantes de l'athlète antique' (Loti, *Journal intime*, January 1878 (unpublished); quoted in Wake, *The Novels of Pierre Loti*, p. 36.

48. Blanch, *Pierre Loti*, pp. 165, 166.

49. Lerner, *Pierre Loti*, p. 77.

50. Blanch, *Pierre Loti*, p. 231.

51. 'Mon métier de marin et mes longs voyages exercent aussi, sur tout ce monde, leur prestige; c'est à qui sera mon ami, à qui sera ma maîtresse' (Pierre Loti, *Un Jeune Officier pauvre* (Paris: Calmann-Lévy, 1923) pp. 114–15.

52. Blanch, *Pierre Loti*, p. 232.

53. 'Ces compagnons que je me suis choisis ont, il est vrai, fait tous les métiers et navigué sous tous les pavillons. . . . C'est une poignée d'hommes que je tiens dans ma main et prêts à me suivre jusque dans le feu' (Loti, *Un Jeune Officier pauvre*, pp. 132–3).

54. Blanch, *Pierre Loti*, p. 219.

55. 'l'immense Péril jaune' (Pierre Loti, *La Troisième Jeunessede Mme Prune* (Paris, Calmann-Lévy, 1928) p. 70).

NOTES TO CHAPTER 3: NINETEENTH-CENTURY ATTITUDES TOWARDS WOMEN

1. 'Loti's interest in remote lands and exotic images is brought forth by the essential dissatisfaction with modern civilization, where the fundamental problems of man's existence are confused and overshadowed by a practical civilization and by a sophisticated culture' (Richards, 'Exoticism in the Works of Pierre Loti', p. 439). Although Richards speaks specifically of Loti, the sentiment is equally valid for any of a number of artists concerned with the exotic.

2. 'de mélancoliques idylles dans des décors de rêve' (Roland Lebel, *Histoire de la littérature coloniale en France* (Paris: Librairie Larose, 1931) p. 69).

3. Ibid., pp. 50ff.

4. 'The exoticist . . . transports himself in imagination outside the actualities of time and space, and thinks that he sees in whatever is past and remote from him the ideal atmosphere for the contentment of his own senses . . . [he] invests remote periods and distant countries with the vibration of his own senses and materializes them in his imagination' (Praz, *The Romantic Agony*, pp. 210–11).

5. 'The person who sets out for distant shores is often seeking spiritual

as well as physical exodus from his normal surroundings; while looking at the mysteries of a foreign land, he may be trying to unravel some of his own inner mysteries' (A. L. Weir, 'Two Views of Exoticism: The Indias of E. M. Forster and Pierre Loti', *Exploration*, 7 (1979) p. 17).

6. Said, *Orientalism*, pp. 2, 3.
7. Said's views, as expressed in this book, are highly controversial, and caused an enormous outpouring of critical discussion within the academic community. For a detailed analysis and devastating critique of Said's interpretation of Orientalism, see Bernard Lewis, 'The Question of Orientalism', *The New York Review of Books*, no. 11 (29 June 1982) pp. 49–56. Nevertheless, there is certainly widespread agreement by scholars that Said's analysis, especially of the pre-twentieth-century writings, contains much merit, although few would agree with the entire argument.
8. Ibid., p. 40.
9. Raymond Schwab, *La Renaissance orientale* (Paris: Payot, 1950).
10. 'Si l'Orient fut pour le Romantisme une source d'inspiration surtout esthétique, l'Islam, lui, fut pour un petit nombre de Romantiques français une préoccupation d'ordre plutôt spirituel et moral' (Moenis Taha-Hussein, *Le Romantisme français et l'Islam* (Beirut, Lebanon: Dar al-Maarif, 1962) p. 8).
11. Ibid.
12. 'est absolument de faire une oeuvre vraie, une oeuvre coloniale, mais bien plutôt de divertir le public, et pour cela il est nécessaire de lui représenter le pays aussi exotiquement que possible' (Lebel, *Histoire de la Littérature coloniale*, p. 80).
13. 'A love of the exotic is usually an imaginative projection of a sexual desire' (Praz, *The Romantic Agony*, p. 207).
14. Said, *Orientalism*, p. 190.
15. Ibid., p. 192.
16. 'Toute l'éducation des femmes doit être relative aux hommes. Leur plaire, leur être utile ou faire aimer et honorer d'eux, les élever jeunes, les soigner grands, les conseiller, les consoler, leur rendre la vie agréable et douce: voilà les devoirs des femmes de tous les temps. Tant qu'on ne remontera pas à ce principe, on s'écartera du but' (Jean-Jacques Rousseau, *Emile*, I, v; quoted in Jean-François Tetu, 'Remarques sur le statut juridique de la femme au XIXe siècle', in *La Femme au XIXe siecle* (Lyon: Presses Universitaires de Lyon, n.d.) p. 75.
17. Theodore Zeldin, *France, 1848–1945*, vol. I: *Ambition, Love, and Politics* (Oxford: Clarendon Press, 1973) p. 345.
18. Ibid., p. 344.
19. Ibid., footnote 2, p. 346.
20. Theodore Stanton, 'France', in Theodore Stanton (ed.), *The Woman Question in Europe* (New York: G. P. Putnam's Sons, 1884) pp. 258–9.
21. Ibid., p. 259.
22. Jules Thabaut, *L'Evolution de la legislation sur la famille* (1913), quoted in Zeldin, *France, 1848–1945*, vol. I, p. 288.

23. Stanton (ed.), *The Woman Question in Europe*, p. 275.
24. James McMillan, *Housewife or Harlot* (New York: St Martin's Press, 1981) p. 15.
25. Zeldin, *France, 1848–1945*, vol. i, footnote 2, p. 346.
26. 'In 1906 68.2% of the male population of all ages worked and 38.9% of the female population' (ibid., p. 351).
27. Ibid., *passim*.
28. Stanton (ed.), *The Woman Question in Europe*, p. 266.
29. J. P. T. Bury, *France, 1814–1840* (New York: A. S. Barnes, 1962) pp. 228–9.
30. William Ellis, *Polynesian Researches. Society Islands, Tutuai Islands and New Zealand* (Rutland, Vt: Charles E. Tuttle, 1969) p. 294.
31. Ibid., Edouard Doty, 'Introduction', p. xii.
32. Colin Newbury, *Tahiti Nui: Change and Survival in French Polynesia, 1767–1945* (Honolulu: University Press of Hawaii, 1980) p. 192.
33. Douglas L. Oliver, *Ancient Tahitian Society*, vol. i (Honolulu: University Press of Hawaii, 1974) p. 361.
34. Ibid., pp. 353–4. The internal quotation is taken from William Bligh, *A Voyage to the South Sea* (London: G. Nicol, 1789).
35. Oliver, *Ancient Tahitian Society*, vol. i, pp. 354–5.
36. Ibid., p. 431; quoted from Johann Reinhold Forster, *Observations Made During a Voyage Round the World on Physical Geography, Natural History and Ethic Philosophy. Part 6: The Human Species* (London: G. Robinson, 1778) p. 422.
37. John E. Eberegbulum Njoko, *The World of the African Woman* (Metuchen, N.J.: Scarecrow Press, 1980) p. 17.
38. Soeur Marie-André du Sacré-Coeur, *La Femme noire en Afrique occidentale* (Paris: Payot, 1939) p. 51.
39. Ibid., p. 84.
40. 'The wealthy farmer acquires a large number of wives – one of the principal forms of conspicuous consumption possible in technologically simple societies' (P. C. Lloyd, *Africa in Social Change* (Baltimore, Md: Penguin Books, 1967) p. 45.
41. Soeur Marie-André du Sacré-Coeur, *La Femme noire*, p. 87.
42. 'tout ce qui est nécessaire à leur subsistance et à leur entretien' (ibid., p. 90).
43. 'Elle peut s'y permettre de grandes libertés, sans que l'époux soit qualifié pour s'en plaindre' (ibid., p. 91).
44. 'L'adultère es réprimé par la coutume, non parce qu'il est en soi une infraction à la loi morale, mais parce qu'il constitue, aux yeux des indigènes, une atteinte au droit de propriété du possesseur de la femme (mari ou fiancé)' (ibid., p. 92).
45. 'L'amour conjugal, fait de grandeur, de tendresse et de force, cet amour qui porte au sacrifice et à l'oubli de soi lorsqu'il s'agit du bonheur de l'époux, ne se rencontre que très exceptionellement en Afrique Occidentale, chez de rares monogames. Il est quelquefois remplacé par la passion aveugle, jalouse, tyrannique qui finit par empoisonner la rivale ou le mari' (ibid., p. 248).
46. Lloyd, *Africa in Social Change*, p. 179.

47. Elizabeth Warnock Fernea and Basima Qattan Bezirgan (eds), *Middle Eastern Muslim Women Speak* (Austin, Tx.: University of Texas Press, 1977) p. xxii.

48. Robertson W. Smith, *Kinship and Marriage in Early Arabia* (London: A. & C. Black, 1903; re-issued by Boston, Mass.: Beacon Press, n.d.). Cited in Fernea and Bezirgan, *Middle Eastern Muslim Women Speak*, p. xxii.

49. Fernea and Bezirgan, *Middle Eastern Muslim Women Speak*, p. xxii.

50. ' "And they [women] have rights similar to those [of men] over them in kindness, and men are a degree above them." Surah ii, 228. "Men are in charge of women, because Allah hath made the one of them to excel the other . . .". Surah iv, 34' (quoted ibid., pp. 9, 16).

51. Elizabeth Cooper, *The Harim and the Purdah* (New York: Century, n.d.) p. 59.

52. ' "Forbidden unto you are your mothers, and your daughters, and your sisters, and your father's sisters, and your mother's sisters, and your brother's daughters and your sister's daughters, and your foster-mothers, and your foster-sisters, and your mothers-in-law, and your step-daughters who are under your protection [born] of your women unto whom ye have gone in . . . And [it is forbidden unto you] that ye should have two sisters together, except what hath already happened (of that nature) in the past." Surah iv, 23' (quoted in Fernea and Bezirgan, *Middle Eastern Muslim Women Speak*, p. 15).

53. Surah iv, Article 3: 'And if ye fear that ye will not deal fairly by the orphans, marry of the women, who seem good to you, two, three or four; and if ye fear that ye cannot do justice (to so many) than one (only)' (ibid., p. 13).

54. Alfred Guillaume, *Islam* (Harmondsworth, Middx: Penguin Books, 1962) p. 71.

55. Ibid., p. 175.

56. Ian C. Dengler, 'Turkish Women in the Ottoman Empire', in Lois Beck and Nikki Keddie (eds), *Women in the Muslim World* (Cambridge, Mass.: Harvard University Press, 1978) pp. 229–30.

57. Surah xxxiii, Article 59 (quoted in Fernea and Bezirgan, *Middle Eastern Muslim Women Speak*, p. 25). Nawal El Saadawi, an ardent Egyptian feminist, feels that men insisted on veiling women to protect themselves against their (feminine) strength and power. 'The fact that men felt the need to prescribe such customs, and to keep the women away from participation in normal life seems to explode the myth of the powerful and the defenceless and weak female. The tyranny exerted by men over women indicates that they had taken the measure of the female's innate strength and needed heavy fortifications to protect themselves against it' (Nawal El Saadawi, *The Hidden Face of Eve*, trs. and ed. Sherif Hetata (London: Zed Press, 1980) p. 100).

58. Raphael Patai, 'The Arab World', in Raphael Patai (ed.), *Women in the Modern World* (New York: Free Press, 1967) p. 110.

59. Tezer Taşkiran, *Women in Turkey*, trs. Nida Tektaş, ed. Anna G. Edmonds (Istanbul: Redhouse Yayinevi, 1976) pp. 33–4.

60. Eliot Grinnell Mears, *Modern Turkey* (New York: Macmillan, 1924) p. 145.
61. Most were content to become 'consumers of luxury goods or leisure-time activities in the Ottoman economy' (Dengler, 'Turkish Women in the Ottoman Empire', p. 236).
62. Ibid., p. 238.
63. Joy Paulson, 'Evolution of the Feminine Ideal', in Joyce Lebra, Joy Paulson and Elizabeth Powers (eds), *Women In Changing Japan* (Boulder, Col.: Westview Press, 1976) p. 10.
64. Herbert Passin, 'Japan', in James S. Coleman (ed.), *Education and Political Development* (Princeton, N.J.: Princeton University Press, 1985) p. 307.
65. Quoted in Paulson, 'Evolution of the Feminine Ideal', p. 11.
66. 'Matsudaira Sadanoba, the Shogunal Chancellor from 1786–93' (quoted in Herbert Passin, *Society and Education in Japan*, Comparative Education Series, Comparative Education Studies (New York: Columbia University Press, 1965) p. 46).
67. Alice Mabel Bacon, *Japanese Girls and Women* (Boston, Mass.: Houghton Mifflin, 1902) pp. 76–7.
68. Lafcadio Hearn, *Japan: An Attempt at Interpretation* (New York: Grosset & Dunlap, 1904) p. 82.
69. Ibid., p. 192.
70. Paulson, 'Evolution of the Feminine Ideal', p. 12.
71. Allen K. Faust, *The New Japanese Womanhood* (New York: George Doran, 1926) p. 31.

NOTES TO CHAPTER 4: LOTI AND WOMEN: A RE-EVALUATION

1. 'Suleima', in Pierre Loti, *Fleurs d'ennui* (Paris: Calmann-Lévy, 1883).
2. 'Cet épisode est une reproduction exacte de celui de la gitane de Fontbruant. Il y a la même pitié pour un être inculte dont les apparences cachent pour Loti une bonté foncière, le même respect implicite de la femme et le même sentiment de la noblesse de son vrai rôle' (Rafter, *La Femme dans l'oeuvre de Pierre Loti*, p. 128).
3. 'Il est infiniment sensible à la tendresse féminine' (George Strem, 'Un Chercheur d'âme, Pierre Loti', *La Revue de l'Université Laval (Québec)*, vol. 14, no. 9 (1960) p. 784).
4. Lesley Blanch, 'Loti-land', *Cornhill Magazine*, vol. 5, no. 168 (1956) p. 392.
5. 'Pour les femmes, cet officier de marine aux aventures exotiques représentait l'amant-type, à la fois ardent et rêveur. Elles se retrouvaient dans ce qu'il exprimait de tendre et de langoureux, de passionné et aussi de joli; elles lui étaient reconnaissantes d'idéaliser l'amour sans oublier la volupté, et d'en faire la suprême raison de vivre' (Robert Traz, *Pierre Loti* (Paris: Librairie Hachette, 1948) p. 164).

6. 'Ses amoureuses . . . pourtant nées aux quatre coins du monde, ont un air de famille: la même passion exclusive qu'achève la mort, les emplit; et si douces elles sont, si fidèles, si résignées à ne comprendre rien de leurs fugaces amants!' (Lucien Duplessy, 'Pierre Loti, a-t-il fait des romans?', *Grande Revue*, December 1925, p. 223).

7. 'Les jeunes filles sont toutes chastes et pures; les jeunes femmes, par contre, ne le sont pas, mais elles rachètent leur manque de chasteté par un profond attachement à leur amant. Toutes sont décrites exclusivement à travers de désir masculin. Elles n'ont pas de vie personnelle et n'ont de prix que par rapport à celui que leur attache l'homme qui les désire' (Leguillon, 'Un aspect de l'amour chez Pierre Loti', p. 46).

8. *Les Désenchantées* provides the exception to prove this 'rule'. The three women, 'Les Désenchantées', appear irreducible; alone among the numerous Oriental heroines, these three women are invested with a certain individuality which appears, at first glance, to defy the usual Loti characterisations. Their apparent differences, however, are only superficial. All three have similar aspirations, share in the same lifestyle, and all die rather than revolt against their condition. Here is a prime example of how Loti's masculine vision reduces feminine participation to supine accord.

9. 'In sexual life itself we see how the simple craving of love that drives men to women is very often overshadowed by their overwhelming inner compulsion to prove their manhood again and again to themselves and others. A man of this type in its more extreme form has therefore one interest only: to conquer. His aim is to have "possessed" many women, and the most beautiful and most sought-after women' (Karen Horney, 'The Dread of Women', in *Feminine Psychology* (New York: W. W. Norton, 1967) p. 145).

10. 'petites barbares', 'deux pauvres petites moumouttes' (Loti, *Mme Prune*, p. 308).

11. 'gaîeté simiesque' (Loti, *Le Mariage de Loti*, p. 16).

12. 'Rieuses petites creatures qui . . . s'ébattaient comme deux poissons-volants' (ibid., pp. 13–14).

13. Loti, *Madame Chrysanthème* (Paris: Calmann-Lévy, n.d.) p. 21.

14. 'comme un chien fidèle à l'excès' (Loti, *Les Désenchantées*, pp. 18–19).

15. 'avec une expression hideuse de bête qu'on a dérangée dans ses amours' (Pierre Loti, *Le Roman d'un Spahi*, p. 55).

16. 'absolument comme il s'y prenait pour gratter la nuque du gros matou calin' (ibid., p. 62).

17. See Sigmund Freud, 'The Tendency to Debasement in Love', *The Standard Edition of the Complete Psychological Works of Sigmund Freud*, trs. and ed. James Strachey (London: Hogarth Press and Institute of Psychoanalysis, 1957) vol. XI, p. 183.

18. 'Comme l'âme de Marguerite, son âme était pure et vierge, bien que son corps d'enfant, acheté par un vieillard, ne le fût déjà plus' (Loti, *Aziyadé*, p. 201).

19. 'petite gitane voleuse' (Loti, *Prime Jeunesse*, p. 147).

20. *Le Mariage de Loti*, p. 4.

21. 'La coquetterie et la gourmandise l'avaient poussée hors du droit chemin' (ibid., p. 56).

22. 'C'était cette Fatou qui depuis quatre ans lui prenait son argent, sa dignité, sa vie!' (Loti, *Roman d'un spahi*, p. 253).

23. Horney, *Feminine Psychology*, p. 146.

24. 'ne nous dit-il pas le vide du discours à travers qui le rapport humain se constitue?' (Roland Barthes, 'Le Nom d'Aziyadé', *Critique* (Paris), 28 (1972) p. 106).

25. 'Se retrouver soi-meme, dans une identité qui est plénitude originelle, c'est bien la fin que n'a cessé de se proposer Loti' (Mario Maurin, 'Pierre Loti et les voies du sacre', *Modern Language Notes*, vol. 81, no. 3 (May 1966) p. 290).

26. 'A l'imitation de Chateaubriand, certains de nos écrivains – Loti et Barrès surtout, – ne voient dans l'utilisation littéraire des thèmes que leur fournit l'étranger qu'un moyen d'enrichir leur sensibilité et d'analyser leur moi: le Japon ou l'Espagne, le Sénégal, Tahiti ou Venise leur offrent certes de splendides paysages et des moeurs curieuses à étudier. *Leur objet essentiel n'en reste pas moins l'observation de leur propre personnalité* (Pierre Jourda, *L'Exotisme dans la littérature française*, I, *Le Romantisme* (Geneva: Slatkine Reprints, 1970) pp. 279–80).

27. 'C'est le journal d'un été de ma vie, auquel je n'ai rien changé; pas même les dates. . . . Bien que le rôle le plus long soit en apparence à madame Chrysanthème il est bien certain que les trois principaux personnages sont *Moi, le Japon et l'Effet* que ce pays m'a produit' (Loti, *Madame Chrysanthème*, p. 1).

28. 'Loti, c'est le héros du roman (même s'il a d'autres noms et même si ce roman se donne pour le récit d'une realité, non d'une fiction). Loti est *dans* le roman (la créature fictive, Aziyadé, appelle sans cesse son amant *Loti*: "Regarde, Loti, et dis-moi . . ."); mais il est aussi en dehors puisque le Loti qui a écrit le livre ne coincide nullement avec le héros Loti: ils n'ont pas même la même identité: le premier Loti est anglais, il meurt jeune; le second Loti, prénommé Pierre, est membre de l'Académie française, il a écrit bien d'autres livres que le récit de ses amours turques' (Barthes, 'Le Nom d'Aziyadé', p. 104).

29. Loti, *Madame Chrysanthème*, p. 46.

30. 'On ne lui [Aziyadé] avait appris aucun principe de morale qui put la mettre en garde contre elle-même' (Loti, *Aziyadé*, p. 210).

31. 'Elle [Rarahu] comprenait vaguement qu'il devait y avoir des abîmes dans le domaine intellectuel, entre Loti et elle-même, des mondes entiers d'idèes et de connaissances inconnues' (Loti, *Le Mariage de Loti*, p. 74).

32. Sigmund Freud, 'A Phobia in a Five-Year-Old Boy', in *Collected Papers*, 3rd edn, trs. Alix and james Strachey (London: Hogarth Press, 1946) vol. III, p. 170).

33. Freud, 'A Case of Obsessional Neurosis', ibid., vol. III, p. 375. Freud maintains that overt hatred is too difficult for the patient to deal with, and so it is displaced by less harmful actions. 'Displacement . . . ensured . . . deriving a considerable advantage' (ibid., p. 336).

34. H. R. Hays, *The Dangerous Sex: The Myth of Feminine Evil* (New York: G. P. Putnam's Sons, 1964) p. 281.
35. 'Ses héros, dont les expériences sont basées très souvent sur les siennes propres, connaissent tous les mêmes sentiments que lui. Au vrai, c'est de Pierre Loti qu'ils tiennent, et ils se ressemblent entre eux' (Millward, *L'Oeuvre de Pierre Loti*, p. 126).
36. 'The neurotic, essentially libidinally fixated character is bound to resist what might dislodge him from his natural tendency toward fixations. These resistances to the awareness of id impulses were said to protect the patient from the consequence acting on them would bring – castration, presumably dreaded by the boy primarily because it would forever preclude the fulfillment of man's ultimate hope: regression through union with the mother or her substitute' (Erwin Singer, *Key Concepts in Psychotherapy* (New York: Basic Books, 1965) p. 230).
37. Hays, *The Dangerous Sex*, p. 44.
38. Quoted ibid., p. 57.
39. According to Hays 'twenty-two versions of this myth have been found in North America alone. It occurs in the mythology of the Siberian tribes and in India and in New Guinea (ibid., p. 55). South Americans, Australians, Hebrews, and Hindus also replicate similar archetypal images.
40. Horney, *Feminine Psychology*, p. 53.
41. Ibid., p. 56.
42. Hays (*The Dangerous Sex*, p. 59) quotes Géza Roheim, 'The Evolution of Culture', *International Journal of Psychoanalysis*, 15 (1934), as the source of this quotation. However I examined this article and was unable to find the citation in it.
43. 'Mais nous croyons qu'il existe en lui un fatal désir de se faire aimer et puis d'en souffrir. Nous verrons par la suite qu'avec les femmes qu'il a aimées, il lui arrive souvent de souffrir moralement. Cet appétit de souffrance nous semble par moments toucher à un état névropathique. C'est là du pur masochisme' (Millward, *L'Oeuvre de Pierre Loti*, p. 52). Millward also cites S. Nacht, *Le Masochisme: Etude Psychanalytique*, 2nd edn (Paris, 1948) p. 61. According to this author, masochism consists of a pathological need for the subject to be loved, but this craving is tied to a need for suffering. This compulsion is so intense that he will reject love without suffering or transform love into suffering. See also Freud, 'A Case of Obsessional Neurosis', p. 321.
44. 'dans ce masochisme qui se manifeste encore dans ce complexe d'insatisfaction, de mécontentement, dans cette impossibilité de se permettre le moindre bonheur sans que quelque chose vienne le troubler' (Millward, *L'Oeuvre de Pierre Loti*, p. 127).
45. 'L'épisode est paradigmatique, car tous les amours de Loti n'en seront que des reprises' (Maurin, 'Pierre Loti et les voies du sacré', p. 301).
46. 'dont le besoin inassouvi me causait une vraie souffrance (Loti, *Prime Jeunesse*, p. 134).

47. 'une certaine *belle gitane*, farouche et inabordable' (ibid.).
48. 'Je sentis très bien que son dernier regard, pour moi tout seul, s'était adouci dans un vague sourire' (ibid., p. 137).
49. 'un vague français mêlé d'espagnol' (ibid., p. 151).
50. 'Jamais encore je n'avais entendu le son de sa voix, quand ma bouche s'appuya éperdument sur la sienne' (ibid., p. 145).
51. 'que se cachait tout le mysticisme de l'Inde' and 'très basanée, couleur des vieilles terres cuites d'Etrurie' (ibid., p. 136).
52. 'avec les petits détours d'un chat qui craint d'effaroucher sa proie' (ibid., p. 144).
53. 'devant une de ces entrées de grotte qui ressemblent à des portiques de temple cyclopéen' (ibid., p. 146).
54. 'Ah! comme je me rappelle encore cette chaude nuit où commença mon envoûtement!' (ibid., p. 139).
55. 'entre les bras fauves de quelqu-un de sa tribu' (ibid., p. 139).
56. 'Je me croyais au milieu du bois inextricables, dans l'obscurité, me frayant à grand'peine un passage parmi des broussailles et des roseaux' (ibid.).
57. 'la belle Gitane, se débattant à mes côtés contre les lianes qui de plus en plus enlaçaient nos pieds' (ibid., pp. 139–40).
58. 'de trouver quelque recoin plus inviolable encore, dans ce ravin dont l'enchevêtrement ombreux était pourtant déjà une suffisante cachette' (ibid., p. 146).
59. 'Pour la première fois depuis seize ans que j'existais, j'avais cruellement la perception très nette de m'avancer *seul*, dans la vie ephémère' (ibid., p. 133).
60. 'Sans doute elle avait deviné mes raffinements, qui étonnaient et charmaient sa sauvagerie' (ibid., p. 147).
61. 'Ce qui fascinait par-dessus tout, c'était ses yeux de profondeur et de nuit, – derrière lesquelles, qui sait, *il n'y avait peut-être rien*' (ibid., p. 136).
62. 'Petite gitane voleuse', 'fille d'une race de parias', 'la dernière des dernières' (ibid., p. 147); 'sa petite main moricaude, experte à commettre des vols dans les fermes aussi bien qu'à tresser des roseaux en paniers' (ibid., p. 145).

NOTES TO CHAPTER 5: LOTI THE EXPLOITER

1. 'La femme-ange est un type nettement romantique. . . . D'autres au contraire voient dans la femme à qui les lie une funeste passion non un ange, mais un démon, à qui une implacable fatalité les a enchaînés pour leur malheur et leur perte' (Paul van Tieghem, *Le Romantisme dans la littérature européenne* (Paris: Editions Albin Michel, 1948) pp. 268, 269).
2. Praz, *The Romantic Agony*, Chapter IV.
3. Anatole Broyard, review of Peter Gay, *The Bourgeois Experience:*

Victoria to Freud, vol. I: *Education of the Senses*, in *New York Times*, 29 December 1983, p. 18.

4. Queen Pomaré and Vaékéhu of Tahiti, Behidjé-hanum, Aziyadé's 'mother', Kadidja, and Aziyadé's old servant, in Pierre Loti, *Fantôme d'orient* (Paris: Ancienne Maison Michel Lévy Frères, 1893).
5. Blanch, *Pierre Loti*, p. 116.
6. Johnson, 'A Reexamination and Revaluation of the Dual Nature . . . of Pierre Loti', p. 32.
7. Lerner, *Pierre Loti*, pp. 47–8.
8. 'le vide écoeurant et l'immense ennui de vivre' (Loti, *Aziyadé*, p. 14).
9. 'Par ennui, mon Dieu, par solitude, j'en étais venu peu à peu à imaginer et à désirer ce mariage. – Et puis, surtout, vivre un peu *à terre*, en un recoin ombreux, parmi les arbres et les fleurs, comme cela était tentant, après ces mois de notre existence que nous venions de perdre aux Pescadores (qui sont des îles chaudes et sinistres, sans verdure, sans bois, sans ruisseux, ayant l'odeur de la Chine et de la mort)' (Loti, *Madame Chrysanthème*, pp. 2–3).
10. 'J'accepte, en fermant les yeux, tout ce qui peut pour une heure combler le vide effrayant de la vie, tout ce qui est une apparence d'amitié ou d'amour' (ibid., p. 40).
11. 'Aziyadé m'a aidé à passer à Salonique mon temps d'exil' (ibid., p. 57).
12. 'L'ennui était venu vite trouver le pauvre Jean. C'était une sorte de mélancolie qu'il n'avait jamais éprouvée, vague, indéfinissable, la nostalgie de ses montagnes qui commençait, la nostalgie de son village et de ses vieux parents tant aimés' (Loti, *Le Roman d'un spahi*, p. 32).
13. 'cette petite âme noire . . . dissimulée et menteuse . . . avec une dose incroyable de malice et de perversité' (ibid., p. 179).
14. 'Jean passait par différentes phases morales: il avait des hauts et des bas; le plus souvent il n'éprouvait plus qu'un vague ennui, une lassitude de toutes choses; et puis, de temps à autre, le mal du pays, qui semblait endormi dans son coeur, le reprenait pour le faire souffrir' (ibid., pp. 178–9).
15. 'Je m'ennuyais, et l'idée m'est venue, pour me distraire, de recourir aux guéchas' (Loti, *Mme Prune*, p. 18).
16. 'n'importe où le sort vous ait exilé, une âme féminine et jeune (dont l'enveloppe soit un peu charmante, car c'est là encore un leurre nécessaire) . . . vous vienne en aide dans la grande solitude' (ibid., p. 36).
17. 'Ils n'avaient pas peur, seulement ils s'ennuyaient' (ibid., p. 71).
18. 'Et ces trois dames s'ennuyaient beaucoup, parce que, tant que durait le jour, elles n'avaient rien à faire' (Loti, *Fleurs d'ennui*, p. 60); 'Tout le jour ces trois dames s'ennuyaient dans leur vieille prison blanche' (ibid., p. 64); 'Elles étaient comme plongées dans une tristesse immense, dans un écoeurement d'abruties, filles d'une race condamnée, subissant des choses fatales avec une résignation morne' (ibid., pp. 64–5).
19. 'Il vit qu'elle était vieille, que son visage était ridé et sa chair

affaissée. – Il s'en détourna avec horreur, la repoussant du pied' (ibid., p. 95).

20. 'garderaient entre elles le secret et la souillure d'un crime' (ibid., p. 74).

21. 'On a toujours tort de chercher à faire de mal aux gens, surtout lorsque ce sont de bons louloups affectueux comme ceux de cette histoire' (ibid., p. 101).

22. 'D'ailleurs il n'y a pas de louis d'or qui puisse payer un baiser spontané qu'une petite fille charmante de seize ans vous donne' (ibid., pp. 339–40).

23. According to Hacioglu, in Turkish Aziyadé means someone who has won his liberty or someone who is free. The word has roots in Arabic and Persian as well; 'Azâd' in Arabic means 'freedom', 'free', or 'liberated', and 'Azadé' in Persian means the same thing. See Necdet Hacioglu, 'La Turquie vue par Pierre Loti' (Dissertation, Université de Poitiers, 1978).

24. 'Local girls were often the closest point of contact between Loti and the indigenous cultures of the places he visited' (Hargreaves, *The Colonial Experience in French Fiction*, p. 34).

25. 'Voilà le secret de l'âme de la musulmane, en Turquie, l'année 1322 de l'hégire. Notre éducation actuelle a amené ce dédoublement de notre être' (Pierre Loti, *Les Désenchantées* (Paris: Calmann-Lévy, 1906) p. 120).

26. 'Loti, pourquoi n'épouserais-tu pas la petite Rarahu du district d'Apiré? Cela serait beaucoup mieux, je t'assure, et te poserait davantage dans le pays' (Pierre Loti, *Le Mariage de Loti* (Paris: Calmann-Lévy, 1924) p. 20.

27. 'quelque chose de *pas humain* qui était effrayant' (Loti, *Le Roman d'un spahi*, p. 164; italics as in the original).

28. 'Le spahi a fait de sa maîtresse noire sa chose, un objet qui pare sa case, un animal qui lui obéit et à qui il impose sa volonté, mais animal qui le désespère car, entre eux, c'est l'abîme des races. Il sait qu'il ne pourra jamais sentir le plaisir à la façon de cet être d'un autre sexe et d'une autre race. Sur le plan des relations sexuelles, Loti ne dédaignait pas les femmes des autres races, mais restait toujours le blanc raffiné. Il a transmis ses préjugés à ses personnages. Le spahi considère la femme noire comme "un fruit gonflé de sucs toxiques rempli de voluptés malsaines", un véritable piège vivant' (Leguillon, 'Un Aspect', pp. 45–6).

29. 'Il était sans force pour se séparer d'elle' (Loti, *Le Roman d'un spahi*, p. 126).

30. 'Ils s'étaient dit qu'une grande fille de quatorze ans n'est plus une enfant, et n'a pas été créée pour vivre seule. . . . Elle n'allait pas se prostituer à Papeete, et c'était là tout ce qu'ils avaient exigé de sa sagesse' (Loti, *Le Mariage de Loti*, p. 26).

31. 'Gardez-vous bien de confondre ce qui est en elle et ce qui est en vous. Toutes nos illusions viennent de là; attribuer ce qui est en nous et nulle part ailleurs à ce qui nous plaît' (Loti, *Aziyadé*, p. 172).

32. 'Si celle-ci n'avait pas été l'héroïne de ses sentiments, une autre

l'aurait fait certainement car Loti était prêt à se lier avec la première femme qui se présenterait à lui: "Si elle ne venait pas . . . une autre prendrait sa place"' (Fallah-Najmeh, 'La Femme musulmane', p. 81, quoting from Loti, *Aziyadé*, p. 84).

33. *Les Désenchantées* does record a fervent relationship, but the 'love' is Platonic and unrealised (see Chapter 6). In *Le Mariage de Loti*, the hero confesses that 'for the first time, she seemed *someone* to me' ['pour la première fois elle me semblait *quelqu'un*'] (pp. 57–8; italics as in original). Although this complimentary reference acknowledges Rarahu's new stature in Loti's eyes, the statement is not a confession of love.

34. Loti, *Aziyadé*, pp. 226, 228.

35. 'qui pourrait bien démêler ce qui vient des sens, de ce qui vient du coeur?' (ibid., p. 227).

36. 'Les plus singulier de l'histoire est encore ceci, c'est que je l'aime. . . . Du plus profond de mon âme, je l'aime et je l'adore' (ibid., pp. 202–3).

37. 'J'étais tout pour elle, le seul, qu'elle eût aimé, et le seul qui l'eût jamais aimée, et j'allais la quitter pour ne plus revenir' (ibid., pp. 258–9).

38. The sanctification of Aziyadé's memory in his Rochefort home certainly points to this.

39. 'Et surtout pourquoi éprouve-t-on ces étranges chocs de rappel, uniquement lorsqu'il s'agit de pays, de lieux ou de temps, que l'amour a touchés avec sa baguette de délicieuse et mortelle magie?' (Loti, *Fantôme d'orient*, p. 9).

40. 'Dans ce rêve obsédant qui, depuis ces dix années, m'est revenu tant de fois, m'est revenu chaque semaine, jamais, jamais je n'ai revu, pas même défiguré ou mort, son jeune visage; jamais je n'ai obtenu, même d'un fantôme, une indication, si confuse qu'elle fût, sur sa destinée' (ibid., p. 17).

41. According to Hacioglu, 'Nedjibé' means a woman of noble stock (see Hacioglu, 'La Turquie vue par Pierre Loti').

42. 'Pendant des années, au cours de ses voyages et des agitations de son existence errante, même au bout du monde, il avait tant de fois dans ses insomnies songé à cela, qui ressemblait aux besognes infaisables des mauvais rêves: au milieu d'un saint cimetière de Stamboul, relever ses humbles marbres qui se désagrégeaient' (Loti, *Les Désenchantées*, p. 197).

43. For a discussion of the role of Stamboul in Pierre Loti's Turkish fiction see my article on this subject in *The Turkish Studies Association Bulletin*, vol. VII, no. 2 (1983) pp. 1–5.

44. 'Il y avait trois ans que Jean Peyral avait mis le pied sur cette terre d'Afrique, – et depuis qu'il était là, une grande transformation s'était faite en lui. Il avait passé par plusieurs phases morales; – les milieux, le climat, la nature, avaient exercé peu à peu sur sa tête jeune toutes leurs influences énervantes; – lentement, il s'était senti glisser sur des pentes inconnues; – et aujourd'hui, il était l'amant de Fatou-gaye, jeune fille noire de race khassonkée, qui avait jeté sur lui je ne sais

quelle séduction, sensuelle et impure, je ne sais quel charme d'amulette' (Loti, *Le Roman d'un spahi*, p. 23).

45. 'Je t'avais prise pour m'amuser; tu n'y as peut-être pas très bien réussi, mais tu as donné ce que tu pouvais, ta petite personne, tes révérences et ta petite musique; somme toute, tu as été assez mignonne, dans ton genre nippon. Et, qui sait, peut-être penserai-je à toi quelquefois, par ricochet, quand je me rappellerai ce bel été, ces jardins si jolis, et le concert de toutes ces cigales (Loti, *Madame Chrysanthème*, p. 317).

46. 'C'est un beau pays que l'Océanie; – de belles créatures, les Tahitiennes; – pas de régularité grecque dans les traits, mais une beauté originale qui plaît plus encore . . . Au fond, des femmes incomplètes qu'on aime à l'égal des beaux fruits, de l'eau fraîche et des belles fleurs' (Loti, *Le Mariage de Loti*, p. 309).

47. 'Qu'est-ce qui peut bien se passer dans sa petite tête? Ce que je sais de son langage m'est encore insuffisant pour le découvrir. D'ailleurs, il y a cent à parier qu'il ne s'y passe rien du tout. – Et quand même, cela me serait si égal!' (Loti, *Madame Chrysanthème*, p. 68).

48. Suetoshi Funaka, '"Le Journal de Nagasaki" et *Mme Chrysanthème* de Pierre Loti", *Etudes de langue et littérature françaises*, vol. xxx (1977) p. 92.

49. 'Nous trouvons dans ce livre des conceptions parfaitement erronées sur le Japon, de l'exotisme trop accentué, des préjugés d'Occidental qui ne sont plus valables de nos jours' (ibid.).

50. 'Ce qu'il a cherché au Japon, ce sont les images qu'il s'est formées du Japon avant d'y venir' (Kôji Nishimoto, 'Loti en face du Japon', *Revue de l'Université Laval*, vol. v, no. 16 (1962) p. 446).

51. For a discussion of Loti's impressions of Turkey and their validity, see Chapter 7.

52. Blanch, *Pierre Loti*, p. 116; see also Hargreaves, *The Colonial Experience in French Fiction*, p. 32.

53. 'The thoughts which contract the strange face of the queen [Queen Vaékéhu] remain a mystery to all, and the secret of her eternal meditations is impenetrable. Is this sadness or brutishness? Does she dream of something or rather of nothing?' ['Les pensées qui contractent le visage étrange de la reine restent un mystère pour tous, et le secret de ses éternelles rêveries est impénétrable. Est-ce tristesse ou abrutissement? Songe-t-elle à quelque chose, ou bien à rien?'] (*Le Mariage de Loti*, p. 108).

54. '"Beaucoup de choses, répondis-je, que toi tu ne peux pas comprendre"' (ibid., p. 151).

55. Loti, ibid., p. 21.

56. Loti, *Aziyadé*, pp. 147–8.

57. 'Le christianisme superficiel des indigènes est resté sans action sur leur manière de vivre, et la dissolution de leurs moeurs dépasse toute idée' (Loti, *Le Mariage de Loti*, pp. 103–4).

58. 'Sa religion est un ténébreux chaos de théogonies vieilles comme le monde, conservées par respect pour les choses anciennes, et d'idées plus récentes sur le bienheureux néant final, apportées de l'Inde à

l'époque de notre Moyen Age par de saints missionaires chinois. Les bonzes eux-mêmes s'y perdent, – et alors, que peut devenir tout cela greffé d'enfantillage et de légèreté d'oiseau, dans la tête d'une mousmé qui s'endort?' (Loti, *Madame Chrysanthème*, pp. 206–7).

59. 'Je perds même mes préjugés d'Occident' (ibid., p. 237).
60. 'Mélange de jeune fille, d'enfant et de diablotin noir, très bizarre petite personne' (Loti, *Roman d'un spahi*, p. 100).
61. 'ébourifée de mouton noir' (ibid., p. 106).
62. 'rusée comme celle d'un jeune singe' (ibid., p. 127).
63. 'Elle avait l'air de s'être coiffée dans la peau d'un porc-épic' (ibid., p. 133).
64. 'Elle était toujours propre comme une chatte noire habillée de blanc' (ibid., p. 137).
65. 'Des mains de Fatou . . . lui causait . . . une vilaine impression de pattes de singe' (ibid., p. 164).
66. 'il l'appellait même, en riant, d'un bizarre nom yolof qui signifiait *"petite fille singe"'* (ibid., p. 165; italics as in the original).
67. 'Jean aimait-il Fatou-gaye? il n'en savait trop rien lui-même, le pauvre spahi. Il la considérait, du reste, comme un être inférieur, l'égal à peu près de son *laobé* jaune; il ne se donnait guère la peine de chercher à démêler ce qu'il pouvait bien y avoir au fond de cette petite âme noire, noire, – noire comme son enveloppe de Khassonkée' (ibid., p. 179).
68. 'Dans tous les pays du Soudan, la femme est placée, vis-à-vis de l'homme, dans des conditions d'infériorité très grande. Plusieurs fois dans le courant de sa vie, elle est achetée et revendue comme un tête de bétail, à un prix qui diminue en raison inverse de la laideur, de ses défauts et de son âge' (ibid., p. 137).
69. 'Mais était-ce puissance d'amulettes, – ou force de l'habitude, – ou inertie de sa volonté endormie par toutes les lourdeurs de l'air? Fatou continuait à le tenir sous sa petite main, – et il ne la chassait point' (ibid., p. 182).
70. 'Elle considère comme très inconvenants ces petits cheveux, et passe chaque matin une heure en efforts tout à fait sans succès pour les aplatir. Ce travail et celui qui consiste à teindre ses ongles en rouge orange sont ses deux principales occupations' (Loti, *Aziyadé*, p. 97).
71. 'que son Dieu n'est pas le même que le tien, et qu'elle n'est pas bien sûre, d'après le Koran, que les femmes aient une âme comme les hommes' (ibid., p. 26).
72. E. E. Calverley, *Islam: An Introduction*, vol. I (Cairo: American University at Cairo, 1958) p. 4.
73. 'That the wives and children of believers share in the joys of Paradise is self-evident for Mohammed, and is especially mentioned in several places' (Tor Andrae, *Mohammed: The Man and his Faith*, trs. Théophil Menzel (New York: Harper, 1960) p. 57).
74. 'Je l'ai prise pour me distraire' (Loti, *Madame Chrysanthème*, p. 68).
75. 'J'en suis venu à penser que tout ce qui me plaît est bon à faire et qu'il faut toujours épicer de son mieux le repas si fade de la vie' (Loti, *Aziyadé*, p. 13).

76. '*Aziyadé* n'est pas un livre tout rose. Ce roman de jeune fille est aussi une petite épopée sodoméenne, marquée d'allusions à quelque chose d'inoui et de ténébreux' (Barthes, 'Le Nom d'Aziyadé', p. 108).
77. 'N'êtes-vous pas content de moi? et qu'ai-je pu vous faire? Sa main tremblait dans la mienne et la serrait plus qu'il n'eût été nécessaire. – *Che volete*, dit-il d'une voix sombre et troublée, *che volete mi?* (Que voulez-vous de moi?) Quelque chose d'inouï et de ténébreux avait un moment passé dans la tête du pauvre Samuel; – dans le vieil Orient tout est possible! . . . Mais depuis cet instant étrange, il est à mon service corps et âme' (Loti, *Aziyadé*, pp. 19, 20).
78. 'Mes soirées se passaient en compagnie de Samuel. J'ai vu d'étranges choses avec lui, dans les tavernes des bateliers' . . . Peu à je m'attachais à lui, et son refus de me servir auprès d'Aziyadé me faisait l'estimer davantage. . . . Mais j'ai vu d'étranges choses la nuit avec ce vagabond, une prostitution étrange, dans les caves où se consomment jusqu'à complète invresse le mastic et le raki' (ibid., pp. 17 and 18).
79. 'Je n'y voyais plus moi-même qu'à travers un nuage, ma tête s'emplissait de pensées étranges et incohérentes. Les groupes, exténués et haletants, passaient et repassaient dans l'obscurité. La danse tourbillonait toujours, et Achmet, à chaque tour, brissait une vitre du revers de sa main. . . . Une à une, toutes les vitres de l'établissement tombaient à terre, et se pulverisaient sous les pieds des danseurs; les mains d'Achmet, labourées de coupures profondes, ensanglantaient le plancher' (ibid., pp. 272–3).
80. 'Loti, les paroles que tu m'as dites, ne les oublie pas; les promesses que tu m'as faites, ne les oublie jamais! Dans ta pensée, crois-tu que je peux être heureux un seul moment sans toi à Constantinople? Je ne le puis pas, et, quand tu es parti, mon coeur s'est brisé de peine' (ibid., pp. 297–8).
81. All the Oriental heroines are not only passionately in love with their Occidental heroes, but they usually initiate the love affairs. Unrequited love is non-existent in this male fantasy land.
82. 'Le respect exagéré que j'ai pour moi-même, m'empêchera toujours de rouler au plus bas, jusqu'à la débauche vulgaire' (Loti, *Un Jeune Officier pauvre*, p. 115). According to Lesley Blanch (*Pierre Loti*, pp. 109–10), Loti's unpublished journal reveals a far greater mutuality of desire between Samuel and himself than was articulated in the book, and she states that Loti's publishers probably prevented him from delineating the actual relationship in the finished novel.
83. 'De jeunes garçons asiatiques, costumées en almées, exécutaient des danses lascives devant un public composé de tous les repris de la justice ottomane, saturnale d'une écoeurante nouveauté. Je demandai grâce pour la fin de ce spectacle, digne des beaux moments de Sodome' (Loti, *Aziyadé*, pp. 68–9).
84. 'Elle ne se doutait pas, la pauvre petite, que ce garçon si jeune de visage avait déjà abusé de toutes les choses de la vie, et ne lui apportait qu'un coeur blasé, en quête de quelque nouveauté originale;

elle s'était dit qu'il devait faire bon être aimée ainsi' (ibid., pp. 200–1).

85. 'Je lui avais déclaré que le lendemain je ne voulais plus d'elle; qu'une autre allait qu'elle-même reviendrait ensuite, et m'aimerait encore après cette humiliation sans en garder même le souvenir' (p. 188).

86. Loti explains that 'sa présence m'était odieuse' (ibid., p. 192), but the only reaction she manifests to his very peculiar behaviour is that she exhibits an evil grin which made him angry ['La grande dame . . . eut un mauvais rire qui me fit monter la colère au visage'], but he reassures himself by stating that 'of the two roles which we had played, the strangest, assuredly, was not mine' ['des deux rôles que nous avions joués, le plus drôle assurément n'était pas le mien'] (ibid., p. 193).

87. Wake, *The Novels of Pierre Loti*, p. 56.

88. 'Mais il la considère comme ma femme et alors c'est sacré. Je crois en sa parole de la manière la plus complète, et j'ai un vrai soulagement, une vraie joie, à retrouver mon brave Yves des anciens jours. Comment donc ai-je pu subir assez l'influence rapetissante des milieux pour le soupçonner et m'en faire un pareil souci mesquin? N'en parlons seulement plus, de cette poupée . . .' (Loti, *Madame Chrysanthème*, pp. 263–4).

89. In the Breton novels, this friendship provides the basis of most of the works.

90. 'Il est peu de gens avec lesquels ce garçon, très renfermé par nature, cause quelquefois d'une manière un peu intime, – mais vous êtes de ces gens-là' (Loti, *Aziyadé*, p. 81).

91. 'Quel bonheur de pouvoir dire tout ce que l'on sent à quelqu'un qui vous comprend *jusqu'à un certain point*, à quelqu'un qui achève votre pensée avec le même mot qui était sur vos lèvres, dont la réplique fait jaillir de chez vous un torrent de conceptions, un flot d'idées. . . . Vous êtes deux intelligences qui s'ajoutent et se complètent' (ibid., pp. 177–8).

92. John, lui, n'est pas comme moi . . . il est d'ailleurs toujours ce même ami fidèle et sans reproche, ce même bon et tendre frère, qui veille sur moi comme un ange gardien et que j'aime de toute la force de mon coeur' (Loti, *Le Mariage de Loti*, p. 7).

93. 'John . . . mon bien-aimé frère John . . . qui éprouvait une surprise douloureuse quand on lui contait mes promenades nocturnes en compagnie de Faimana' and 'il était disposé à tout pardonner à son frère Harry, quand il s'agissait d'elle' (ibid., p. 27).

94. 'Mon frère John . . . passait au milieu des fêtes de là-bas comme une belle figure mystique, inexplicable pour les Tahitiennes qui jamais ne trouvaient le chemin de son coeur, ni le côté vulnérable de sa pureté de néophyte' (ibid., p. 119).

95. 'Et puis elle continue à rire, – et ce rire très particulier dit clairement le vilain métier qu'elle a déjà commencé à faire' (Loti, *Fleurs d'ennui*, p. 323).

96. 'Une pudeur me retient pourtant, surtout devant Plumkett; il y voit

toujours trop clair, lui, dans tout ce que je voudrais cacher. Et puis, ces sortes d'amour-là, qu'il faut subir, me confondent et me font douter de tout' (ibid., p. 326).

97. 'Il apprit donc que Mélek, depuis quelques jours, avait entrepris des prières et un evoûtement pour obtenir sa mort, – un peu comme enfantillage et plus encore pour tout de bon, s'étant imaginée qu'il incarnait une influence hostile et maintenait André en défiance contre elles' (Loti, *Les Désenchantées*, p. 244).

98. 'Jean ne sentait pas sa force dans ces moments de fureur. Il avait de ces violences un peu sauvages des enfants qui ont grandi dans les bois. Il frappait rudement sur le dos nu de Fatou, marquant des raies d'où jaillissait le sang, et sa range s'excitait en frappant' (Loti, *Le Roman d'un spahi*, p. 247).

99. Ibid., p. 253. See also Praz, *The Romantic Agony*, p. 152: 'This necessity of believing the lover to be a monstrous creature is a characteristic of sadism.'

100. 'Quand il la battait, elle aimait presque cela maintenant, parce qu'il n'y avait guère que dans ces moments-là qu'il la touchait, et qu'elle pouvait le toucher, elle, en se serrant contre lui pour demander grâce' (Loti, *Le Roman d'un spahi*, p. 255).

101. 'J'avais mandé par Ariitéa pour lui faire société pendant ce lunch officiel, – et la pauvre petite Rarahu, qui n'était venue que pour moi, m'attendait longtemps sur le pont, pleurant en silence de se voir ainsi abandonnée. Punition bien sévère que je lui avais infligée là, pour un caprice d'enfant qui durait depuis la veille et lui avait déjà fait verser des larmes' (Loti, *Le Mariage de Loti*, p. 169).

102. 'Did he even contemplate such a hare-brained scheme? I find no mention of it in his letters or journal, although yearnings for Aziyadé are a constant thread' (Blanch, *Pierre Loti*, p. 148).

103. 'Oublie Loti, qui porte malheur à ceux qui l'approchent. Avec Osman Effendi, tu auras des esclaves, des jardins, un rang parmi les femmes de ton pays et ta place d'épouse dans le monde invisible des harems. Tandis qu'avec moi! . . . Si même toutes les impossibilités étaient vaincues, as-tu songé à ce que ce serait d'être ma femme? Venir seule, en fugitive, dans un pays lointain, où personne ne comprendrait ton langage. . . . Aller sans voile, comme une femme 'franque'; partager ma misère, prendre ta part des durs travaux de la maison, comme le font tes servantes, et, pendant les années où je serai au loin, à voyager sur les mers, rester seule. Durant de longs hivers, plus longs que ceux de Stamboul, dans ce pays plus rapproché de l'étoile froide, ne plus voir ni le ciel bleu, ni ta patrie, ni tes semblables, ne plus même entendre une voix amie. . . . Mais si tu acceptes tout cela, ma bien-aimée, si tu aimes tant que tu veuilles tout supporter, si tu veux fuir . . . alors viens, je t'adore et je t'attends' (Loti, *Un Jeune Officier pauvre*, pp. 200–1).

104. 'Oui, vues de dos, elles sont mignonnes; elles ont, comme toutes les Japonaises, des petites nuques délicieuses. Et surtout elles sont drôles, ainsi rangées en bataillon. En parlant d'elles, nous disons:

"Nos petits chiens savants", et le fait est qu'il y a beaucoup de cela dans leur manière' (Loti, *Madame Chrysanthème*, p. 84).

105. 'J'ai rencontré le jouet que j'avais peut-être vaguement désiré toute ma vie: un petit chat qui parle' (ibid., p. 27).

106. '– *Toi tout à fait même chose comme singe! Et Fatou, très vexée: – Ah! Tjean! Toi n'y a pas dire ça, mon blanc! D'abord, singe, lui, n'y a pas connaît manière pour parler, – et moi connais très bien!*' (Loti, *Roman d'un spahi*, p. 166; italics as in original). Her pigeon French is outrageous; Loti endows her with minimal linguistic prowess, even though she has been living with French-speaking Jean for three years.

107. 'Mais comment donc suis-je redevenu tout à coup aussi calme, presque distrait? Il semble que je ne comprends plus bien, que je n'y suis plus. Qu'est-ce donc qui m'a fermé le coeur d'une façon si inattendue?' (Loti, *Fantôme d'orient*, pp. 189–90).

108. 'Je reprends peu à peu conscience des choses; je souffre plus simplement, je comprends d'une manière plus humaine et plus douloureuse, le frisson me revient, le vrai frisson d'infinie tristesse' (ibid., p. 227).

109. 'Quand nous mourons, ce n'est que le commencement d'une série d'autres anéantissements partiels, nous plongeant toujours plus avant dans l'absolue nuit noire. Ceux qui nous aimaient meurent aussi; toutes les têtes humaines, dans lesquelles notre image ètait à demi conservée, se désagrègent et retournent à la poussière; tout ce qui nous avait appartenu se disperse et s'émiette; nos portraits, que personne ne connaît plus, s'effacent; – et notre nom s'oublie; et notre génération achève de passer' (ibid., p. 218).

110. 'Oh! comment dire le charme de ce lieu qui s'appelle la Corne d'Or! Comment le dire, même par à peu près: il est fait de mes joies inquiètes et de mes angoisses, mêlées à de l'ombre d'Islam; il n'existe sans doute que pour moi seul' (ibid., p. 101).

111. 'Dans sa mémoire à lui seul, mais rien que là, persistait encore la jeune image, et, quand il serait mort, aucun reflet ne resterait nulle part de ce que fut sa beauté, aucune trace du monde de ce que fut son âme anxieuse et candide' (Loti, *Les Désenchantées*, p. 101).

NOTES TO CHAPTER 6: THE EXPLOITER EXPLOITED

1. 'l'essor déréglé pris par ce jeune esprit' (Loti, *Les Désenchantées*, p. 21).
2. 'trois Pérotes parlant ensemble, cela eût fait songer tout de suite au Jardin d'acclimation, côté des cacatoès' (ibid., p. 111).
3. 'les germes de la mort' (ibid., p. 413).
4. 'Le secret désenchantement des femmes de harem ou d'ailleurs, c'est de rêver d'eunuque devant un mâle, et si elles ne soupirent pour un mâle devant des eunuques. La petite Djénane, bien entendu, ne manque pas à la série et elle finit part se tuer, si lasse de n'étreindre que du vent. Paix à tes cendres petite sotte! En France, on est moins

poupés de bazar que toi et nous lisons nos grands littérateurs sans perdre la tête!' (*Mercure de France*, 15 September 1906, cited in Lefêvre, *Les Désenchantées de Pierre Loti*).

5. Jacques Legrand in 'Clefs pour Les Désenchantées', *Cahiers Pierre Loti*, no. 68 (December 1968) pp. 21–32, argues that the entire novel is a reworking of the Orpheus legend, with Loti/Orpheus attempting to find Djénane/Aziyadé/Eurydice by crossing the Bosphorus/Styx.

6. 'de petites bêtes sensuelles . . . la connaissance qu'il a d'elles est toute spirituelle et il semble chercher et d'écrire autre chose que le pittoresque et le sensuel' (André Chaumeix, *Le Journal des Débats*, 5 August 1906, pp. 101, 93–4).

7. 'Il n'a pas écrit là ses convictions personnelles, d'après les témoignages directs de ses yeux à lui. Ce n'est pas sa pensée qu'il nous livre: c'est un récit de second main, un plaidoyer qu'il a écouté et qu'il a reproduit' (Claude Farrère, 'Pierre Loti', *La Revue Maritime*, February 1950, p. 151).

8. Marc Hélys was a male pseudonym for Mme Marie Léra. 'One of the many indications that this generation [women born after 1800, publishing after 1840] saw the will to write as a vocation in direct conflict with their status as women is the appearance of the male pseudonym' (Showalter, *A Literature of their Own*, p. 19). In addition to masking their sex in order to 'participate in the mainstream of literary culture', 'the pseudonym also protected women from the righteous indignation of their own relatives' (p. 58). It is interesting that a woman who was advocating such a strong feminist position would need to disguise her authorship under a male pseudonym, and it is ironic that a male author would be taken in by a female who posed as a male in her published work.

9. 'Mon travail exigeait une liberté plus grande que n'en pouvait offrir une maison turque' (Marc Hélys, *L'Envers d'un roman: le secret des Désenchantées* (Paris: Perrin, 1923) p. 2); my translation: henceforth all translations from this work will be mine).

10. Ibid., p. 6.

11. 'Leur père répétait souvent avec orgueil que ses enfants n'avaient pas une goutte de sang turc' (ibid., p. 3).

12. 'Mais grâce à leur vive et souple intelligence, le tout ensemble composait un esprit à facettes extrêmement brillant' (ibid., p. 4).

13. 'Je m'étais déjà rendu compte qu'elles étaient loin de représenter le type de la jeune fille turque d'alors' (ibid., p. 6). Lucy Garnett in *Turkey of the Ottomans* (New York: Charles Scribner's Sons, 1911) speaks of the women in *Les Désenchantées* as being 'frivolous' and 'foolishly sentimental'. According to her, Turkish women actually desired reforms 'of a sensible and thoroughly practical character'. They desired educational reform *prior* to social reform, and their increased political-social awareness was self-imposed rather than Occidentally inspired.

Hélys also admitted that the few full-blooded Turkish women she met had received a fine Moslem education (corroborating the findings in Chapter 3, pp. 20–1), but she did not emphasise this in her letter to the famous author.

14. 'Rien n'a été exagéré quant à la popularité de Pierre Loti parmi les femmes turques. Toutes en avaient la tête tournée, jusqu'à celles qui ne comprenaient pas le français, et qui n'avaient même jamais lu ses livres traduits en turc' (Hélys, *L'Envers d'un roman*, p. 8).

15. 'Il avait eu l'art de s'envelopper de mystère et de paraître inaccessible. On le disait d'approche plus difficile que le Sultan' (ibid., p. 9).

16. 's'il faisait beau (ces derniers mots soulignés), il passerait à l'heure dite au café pour ne pas vous faire de peine, au cas ou ce serait sérieux' (ibid., pp. 15–16).

17. In *Les Désenchantées*, Djénane unveils herself in a fictional fulfilment of Loti's desires. Marc Hélys took pains to indicate that she never unmasked herself. Lefêvre in *Les Désenchantées de Pierre Loti* explains that the reason for Hélys' veil was her fear of being recognised. Furthermore, she points out that Marc Hélys was not so young any more, and she wanted Loti to retain an illusion of youth (pp. 44–5).

18. 'Vraiment nous étions bien étonnées. Nous savions d'avance que Pierre Loti parlait peu, mais nous ne nous attendions tout de même pas à une pareille pauvreté de conversation' (Hélys, *L'Envers d'un roman*, p. 27).

19. 'si nous faisions sur son compte quelque réflexion désobligeante' (ibid., p. 26).

20. 'A en semer ainsi les morceaux à travers le monde, il ne doit plus vous en rester' (ibid.).

21. 'arranger de jolis souvenirs pour Pierre Loti' (ibid., p. 200).

22. 'Je *voulais* que Loti s'émût pour ces femmes de Turquie . . . ; Je lui parlai du livre à faire. Avait-il *senti* notre âme?' (ibid., p. 177).

23. 'Et Neyr ajoutait: "Comme il ne peut pas inventer en dehors de lui-même, il faut inventer pour lui." "Mais par rapport à lui, ajoutais-je. Il le faut pour qu'il sente, et qu'il soit ému" ' (ibid., p. 195).

24. 'Nous avions envie de voir comment il faisait ses livres. Nous pensions qu'il allait vouloir vivre un roman, que nous n'aurions qu'à suivre et à lui donner la réplique. Le roman eût été fini tout de suite, si nous n'avions pas nous-mêmes fait naître les incidents. Car lui ne fournissait rien' (ibid., p. 9).

25. 'Et pour ce livre-là, Pierre Loti avait besoin de tout ce que nous lui donnions. Avec tout son génie, il ne poussédait pas le don de pénétrer dans les autres âmes' (ibid., p. 200).

26. Lefêvre in *Les Désenchantées de Pierre Loti* also reproduced the two documents side by side, which facilitates comparison.

27. 'peut . . . aider ses biographes future et ses critiques à mieux préciser son originalité . . . . On y surprendra sur le vif la manière dont Loti compose, l'art subtil et charmant avec lequel il transforme les éléments fournis par la réalité, et les enveloppe d'une poésie prestigieuse' (Hélys, *L'Envers d'un roman*, p. 282).

28. 'Mais pour devenir son ami de demain, il vous faut, Loti, apprendre à voir en elle *autre chose qu'un joli souvenir de voyage, étape enchantée*

dans votre vie d'artiste à la poursuite d'émotions nouvelles. Elle ne sera plus désormais pour vous l'enfant vers qui vous êtes penché, ni l'amante aisément heureuse par l'aumône de votre tendresse . . . le temps est venu pour vous de *chercher et de peindre dans l'amour autre chose que le pittoresque'* (Hélys, *L'Envers d'un roman*, pp. 32–3).

29. 'Mais peut-etre à cause de cela, ai-je mieux su parler des Musulmanes à un Européen' (ibid., p. 76).

30. 'Il se sentait bien plus proche d'elle [Djénane] que de Zennour et de Nouryé. C'est qu'ils avaient les même façons de sentir, étant de la même race' (Lefêvre, *La Vie Inquiète de Pierre Loti*, p. 204).

31. Loti was always extremely class-conscious. Among his friends and acquaintances he was particularly proud of his connections with royalty. *L'Exilée*, the story of the last days of the Queen Carmen Silva of Roumania, eulogised this woman, whom he considered a good friend. He was extremely proud of his association with Sultan Abdul Hamid, and exulted in his non-fiction in the many venerable and royal homes into which he was accepted during his travels.

32. 'J'avais grand besoin de gagner un peu d'argent, car mes voyages à Constantinople m'en avaient coûté, et notre roman m'absorbait depuis plus d'un an au détriment de tout travail. Sans compter – comme Neyr disait en riant – tout ce que nous avions dépensé en timbres, en belles blouses et en fleurs!' (Hélys, *L'Envers d'un roman*, p. 246).

33.

Et voici comment j'imaginais votre livre: un homme a écrit un jour un livre où il a mis son coeur avec ses souvenirs de jeunesse. Puis les souvenirs se sont succédé; les amours aussi. Il est devenu sceptique, et la vie l'a gâté et blasé.

Un jour, en France, dans sa vie parisienne, il reçoit une lettre écrite dans un harem. Il avait presque oublié. La lettre lui raconte que le temps a marché, que la recluse orientale n'est plus une poupée. On lui décrit une vie autre. On lui exprime des pensées, des rêves, des douleurs . . . Il veut enfin voir, connaître ses correspondantes. Il est curieux de sensations. C'est un dilettante.

Il retourne à Stamboul et y cherche sa jeunesse, ses impressions de fraîcheur, ses enthousiasmes. Il connaît enfin celle qui lui écrit.

Je n'en ferais pas un de ces êtres fatals qui sèment le malheur et s'en vont. J'en ferais seulement un artiste, un dilettante, passionné d'impressions nouvelles et exquises.

Et que peut-il arriver si ce n'est l'amour? Mais l'amour d'elle: pas de lui. Il n'est qu'artiste; il aime la vie belle et jolie. Cette aventure le charme parce qu'elle lui révèle un monde inconnu. Il irait volontiers jusqu'au bout de l'aventure; mais ce ne serait pour lui qu'une aventure.

Qu'une Turque aille ou non jusqu'au bout de son amour, la fin de l'histoire est la fuite ou la mort. Mais notre héros ne peut déranger sa vie: il est marié. Et mon héroïne est trop fière pour s'en aller avec lui et n'être pas sa maîtresse.

Elle mourra donc; non pas de cet homme, mais étouffée par ses

rêves, brisée par les entraves qui l'enserrent et ne lui laissent pas le moyen de *se consoler de l'amour par l'action.* [C'est Hélys qui souligne]
  Une partie de votre roman serait en lettres; le reste en fragments de journal. Les vides, le côté qui se rapporterait à la vie musulmane, nous vous l'enverrions. Vous n'auriez qu'à le récrire. Nous y ferions vivre une famille. Tout y serait vrai, sauf les détails extérieurs. Et vous auriez ainsi la vie intime de l'Orient racontée par les Orientales. (Ibid., pp. 181–2)

34. Ibid., p. 41.
35. Hélys sent a letter dated 13 December 1904 to Loti sketching a plan for his possible novel. 'This letter has been used in part by Pierre Loti in dialogue form, page 291 of *Les Désenchantées*' ['Cette lettre a été en partie utilisée par Pierre Loti sous forme de dialogue à la page 291 des *Désenchantées*'] (ibid., p. 183).
36. A long, involved letter Leyla sent him to explain the absence of social classes in Turkey (about four pages) became a third of a page anecdote in the novelist's text (ibid., p. 210).
37. Ibid., p. 79.
38. See the last letter, ibid., Chapter v.
39. The initial letter which the three young women sent to Loti in *Les Désenchantées* was signed 'Mme Zahidé', clearly a near-anagram for Aziyadé.
40. See ibid., pp. 74–89 on the wedding day, its preparations and festivities; pp. 93–103 on impressions of Stamboul, its populace, and the cemeteries; pp. 276–9 for a description of harem life.
41. Stamboul refers to the European part of Constantinople.
42. 'Mais, à cette heure, il aimait avec détresse tout ce Stamboul, dont les milliers de feux du soir commençaient à se refléter dans la mer; quelque chose qui flottait dans l'air au-dessus de la ville immense et diverse, sans doute une émanation d'âmes féminines, – car dans le fond c'est presque toujours cela qui nous attache aux lieux ou aux objets, – des âmes féminines qu'il avait aimées et qui se confondaient' (ibid., p. 407).
43. On the eve of Djénane's wedding, the receipt of Lhéry's letter eclipses the forthcoming marriage. 'His letter . . . was [such] an event in their cloistered life that, up to the great crushing catastrophe of marriage, nothing ever happened' ['Une lettre de lui écrite à l'une d'elles était un événement dans leur vie cloîtrée où, jusqu'à la grande catastrophe foudroyante du mariage, jamais rien ne se passe'] (ibid., p. 30). Even Hélys, in her most purple passage, never equated marriage with a 'great crushing catastrophe'.
44. We have seen this pattern in all the other Oriental novels as well.
45. 'Lettres de femmes, pour la plupart, les unes signées, les autres non, apportant à l'écrivain l'encens des gentilles adorations intellectuelles' (ibid., p. 3).
46. 'et les pauvres lettres s'entassaient, pour être noýes bientôt sous le flot des suivantes et finir dans l'oubli' (ibid., p. 4).
47. ' "parce que vous m'avez fait une gentille déclaration d'amitié

intellectuelle! Quel enfantillage! J'en reçois bien d'autres, allez, et ça ne m'émotionne pas du tout' " (ibid., p. 227).

48. Loti defines a 'désenchantée' in two ways: as one 'discouraged with life, not desiring anything any more, not waiting for anything any more, but resigned with an unalterable gentleness; a creature full of weariness and of tenderness' ['Une désenchantée dans les deux sens de ce mot-là, une découragée de la vie, ne désirant plus rien, n'attendant plus rien, mais résignée avec une douceur inaltérable; une créature toute de lassitude et de tendresse'] (ibid., p. 260).

49. Karen Horney in her discussion of narcissism provides one insight into Loti's emphasis on his popularity when she ponts out 'a person with pronounced narcissistic trends, though incapable of love, nevertheless needs people as a source of admiration and support', *New Ways in Psychoanalysis* (New York: W. W. Norton, 1939) pp. 88–9).

50. 'La pauvre petite Mélek sans doute va mourir, vaincue par tant de surexcitation nerveuse, de révolte, d'épouvante que lui a causé ce nouveau mariage' Loti, *Les Désenchantées*, p. 385.

51. Fetterley, *The Resisting Reader*, p. 48.

52. 'non seulement pour chacun de nous celle où il faudra mourir, mais celles après qui verront tomber les derniers de notre génération, finir l'Islam et disparaître nos races au déclin' (Loti, *Les Désenchantées*, p. 411).

53. ' "Et elle aurait vécu, si elle était restée la petite barbare, la petite princesse des plaines d'Asie! Elle n'aurait rien su du néant des choses. C'est de trop penser et de trop savoir, qui l'a empoisonnée, chaque jour un peu. C'est l'Occident qui l'a tuée, André. Si on l'avait laissée primitive et ignorante, belle seulement, je la verrais là près de moi, et j'entendrais sa voix" ' (ibid., p. 428).

54. 'Sur les ailes de l'ennui, Loti volera de l'inanité de l'amour, à la vanité de toute choses, à l'horreur du néant' (Serban, *Pierre Loti*, p. 108).

55. Richards, 'Exoticism in the Works of Pierre Loti', p. 103.

56. 'Car, vous aussi, André, vous ne m'oublierez plus' (Loti, *Les Désenchantées*, p. 45). 'Les jours qui passaient, sans autre appel de ces inconnues, lui rendaient presque douloureuse l'idée qu'il ne réentendrait sans doute jamais la voix de Zahidé, d'un timbre si étrangement doux le voile' (ibid., p. 129). 'Oh! André, dans des âmes longtemps comprimées comme les nôtres, si vous saviez ce qu'est un sentiment idéal, fait d'admiration et de tendresse' (ibid., pp. 269–70).

57. 'Il les (les lettres) conservait précieusement, car elles lui rappelaient des minutes délicieuses, une amitié qu'il n'oublierait jamais' (Hélys, *L'Envers d'un roman*, p. 117).

58. 'Dans leur cerveau, composé de matière neuve ou longtemps reposée, tout germait à miracle, comme, en terrain vierge, les hautes herbes folles et les jolies fleurs véneneuses' (Loti, *Les Désenchantées*, p. 32).

59. 'Voilà, dit Djénane en riant, vous avez voulu connaitre des Orientales, et bien! c'est ainsi que nous sommes. Dés qu'on gratte un peu le vernis: des petites barbares! (ibid., p. 244).

60. 'Oh! quelqu'un avec qui ces pauvres créatures oubliées, humiliées, pourraient parler, échanger leurs petites, conceptions, le plus souvent craintives et innocentes!' (ibid., p. 264).
61. 'comme dans la fièvre de composer' (ibid., p. 11).
62. 'Sans doute, une mère n'était point dans cette maison pour veiller aux lectures, modérer le surchauffage de ce jeune cerveau' (ibid., p. 11).
63. 'Il comprit alors que, depuis un moment, il lui faisait de la peine en contrecarrant avec demi-moquerie ses petites idées littéraires, qu'elle s'était acquises toute seule, avec tant d'effort et parfois avec une intuition merveilleuse' (ibid., p. 246).
64. 'Et aujourd'hui, causant par miracle avec un homme d'Occident, et un homme au nom connu, elles se trouvaient de niveau; et lui, les traitant comme des égales, comme des intelligences, comme des âmes, ce qui leur apportait une sorte de griserie de l'esprit jusque-là inéprouvée' (ibid., p. 181).
65. 'Il parut à André qu'elles avaient l'âme à la fois haute et naïve, ces deux demi-vieilles filles; du reste, distinguées et supérieurement instruites, mais avec un exaltation romanesque un peu surannée en 1904' (ibid., p. 313).
66. Fallah-Najmeh, 'La Femme musulmane', p. 138.
67. Odalisk is derived from the Turkish word 'oda' meaning room, and 'lik' which is a suffix representing function. An odalisk was a woman whose function it was to remain in the bedroom.
68. Garnett, *Turkey of the Ottomans*, p. 241.
69. Demetra Vaka, *Haremlik* (Boston, Mass.: Houghton Mifflin, 1909) p. 150.
70. Garnett, *Turkey of the Ottomans*, p. 241.
71. Halide Edib, *Turkey Faces West* (New Haven, Conn.: Yale University Press, 1930) pp. 129–30.
72. See *Les Désenchantées de M. Pierre Loti*, published by Lutfi Bey Fikri (Cairo, 1907), cited in Lefêvre, *Les Désenchantées de Pierre Loti*, p. 110.
73. Lutfi Fikri Bey, ibid.
74. Sefer Bey, in *La Revue des deux mondes*, September 1909: 'Non, M. Lhéry, la femme qui vous a écrit n'est pas la musulmane de l'an 1332 . . . elle peut être le produit d'une très brillante imagination . . . elle peut être Française, Anglaise, Allemande ou Américaine, mais Turque, jamais!'
75. Garnett, *Turkey of the Ottomans*, p. 241.
76. 'Mais je savais que ce que je pouvais écrire noi-même ne porterait pas sur le grand public comme un livre de Pierre Loti' (Hélys, *L'Envers d'un roman*, p. 200).
77. 'J'obéis à un sentiment bien naturel de fierté et de joie d'avoir collaboré, inconnue, à une oeuvre très belle' (ibid., Preface).
78. Ibid., p. 282.

NOTES TO CHAPTER 7: CONCLUSION

1. 'Loti owes very little, if anything, to books (his famous quip: "je ne lis jamais" is fundamentally true) and nearly everything to his soul and nature' (Pierre Brodin, 'Should We Forget Pierre Loti?', *American Society Legion of Honor Magazine*, 33 (1962) p. 104).

2. Only in *Le Roman d'un spahi* is Jean Peyral rejected by Cora, the mulatto woman, and it is noteworthy that this is the only Oriental novel written in the third person where the hero is not named Loti.

3. Marc Hélys was a member of the audience.

4. 'un meeting de Peaux-Rouges qui venaient de se parer pour la danse au scalp!' (Loti, 'La Femme Turque', in *Quelques aspects du vertige mondial* (Paris: Ernest Flammarion, 1917) p. 164).

5. 'que le rêve de quelques-unes d'entre elles, déjà un peu déséquilibrées par votre exemple, serait, hélas! d'oser se coiffer comme vous' (ibid., p. 166).

6. One woman who claimed she was the first female to read *Aziyadé* initially revolted against the sequestration of women, but later died veiled, anti-Western, and surrounded by Islamic 'priests' and dervishes (ibid., pp. 170–1).

7. The anecdote Loti relates here concerns Khadidjé-Sultane, the beautiful daughter of Sultan Murad, who was overthrown by his brother Sultan Abdul Hamid. The latter raised his daughter and his niece together and permitted both of them to choose their husbands. The cousins celebrated their nuptials together, and then moved into adjoining palaces which the Sultan had had built for them. The two couples were inseparable. Khadidjé-Sultane, however, bent upon avenging her father's death, ensnared the princess's husband with her beauty, convincing him to poison her cousin while she promised to free herself from her spouse so the lovers could marry. The plot failed and the two culprits were apprehended and imprisoned in Yildiz Palace, never to be seen again. What is most interesting about this tale is that Loti cites it as 'typical'. [J'ai rapporté cette histoire parce qu'elle m'a paru typique.'] (Ibid., p. 178). Loti never indicates of what it is 'typical', but the listener/reader is left with the impression that the anecdote is illustrative of the practices of modern Oriental women, once they are allowed some freedom of choice in finding their husbands.

8. 'Conseillez-leur de ne pas courir trop vite dans les routes inconnues qui mènent à l'avenir' (ibid., p. 181).

9. 'Et je dis avec eux, mais non sans inquiétude: oui, ouvrez toutes les cages, ouvrez tous les harems. Cependant ne les ouvrez pas trop vite, de peur que les jeunes oiseaux prisonniers ne prennent un vol éperdu, avant de bien savoir encore où les conduiront leurs ailes inexpérimentées et fragiles' (ibid., p. 182).

10. See Chapter 3.

11. 'plutôt trop instruites à mon gré' (ibid., p. 172).

12. 'Un de leur grande charme, sans doute, c'est qu'en y regardant de près, on retrouve en elles sous ce prodigieux vernis de modernisme, des Orientales quand même' (ibid., p. 172).

Bibliography

PRIMARY SOURCES

Works Cited

Loti, Pierre, *Aziyadé* (Paris: Calmann-Lévy, 1879).
——, *Correspondance inédits (1865–1904)*, ed. Nadine Duvignau and N. Serban (Paris: Calmann-Lévy, 1906).
——, *Les Désenchantées* (Paris: Calmann-Lévy, 1906).
——, *Fantôme d'orient* (Paris: Ancienne Maison Michel Lévy-Frères, 1893).
——, *Figures et choses qui passaient* (Paris: Calmann-Lévy, 1898).
——, *Fleurs d'ennui* (Paris: Calmann-Lévy, 1883).
——, *Un Jeune Officier pauvre*, ed. Samuel Loti-Viaud (Paris: Calmann-Lévy, 1923).
——, *Journal intime (1878–1881)*, ed. Samuel P. Loti-Viaud (Paris: Calmann-Lévy, 1925).
——, *Lettres à Mme Juliette Adam (1880–1922)* (Paris: Plon, Nourrit, 1924).
——, *Le Livre de la pitié et de la mort* (Paris: Calmann-Lévy, n.d.).
——, *Madame Chrysanthème* (Paris: Calmann-Lévy, n.d.).
——, *Le Mariage de Loti* (Paris: Calmann-Lévy, 1924).
——, *The Marriage of Loti*, trs. Wright and Eleanor Frierson (Honolulu: University Press of Hawaii, 1976).
——, *Prime Jeunesse* (Paris: Calmann-Lévy, 1919).
——, *Quelques aspects du vertige mondial* (Paris: Ernest Flammarion, 1917).
——, *Le Roman d'un enfant* (Paris: Calmann-Lévy, n.d.).
——, *Le Roman d'un spahi* (Paris: Calmann-Lévy, 1881).
——, *La Troisième Jeunesse de Mme Prune* (Paris: Calmann-Lévy, 1928).

Works Consulted

Loti, Pierre, *Au Maroc* (Paris: Calmann-Lévy, 1893).
——, *Le Désert* (Paris: Calmann-Lévy, 1894).
——, *La Galilée* (Paris: Calmann-Lévy, 1894).
——, *L'Inde sans les anglais* (Paris: Calmann-Lévy, 1899).
——, *Jérusalem* (Paris: Calmann-Lévy, 1895).
——, *Journal intime de Pierre Loti à Tahiti* (Papeete: Société des Etudes Océaniennes de Papeete, 1934).
——, *Matelot* (Paris: Calmann-Lévy, 1893).
——, *Mon Frère Yves* (Paris: Calmann-Lévy, 1883).
——, *La Mort de Philae* (Paris: Calmann-Lévy, 1907).
——, *La Mort de notre chère France en orient* (Paris: Calmann-Lévy, 1920).
——, *Pêcheur d'Islande*, ed. James F. Mason (New York: Henry Holt, 1920).

SECONDARY SOURCES

Works and Articles Cited

Andrae, Tor, *Mohammed: The Man and his Faith*, trs. Théophil Menzel (New York: Harper, 1960).

Bacon, Alice Mabel, *Japanese Girls and Women* (Boston, Mass.: Houghton Mifflin, 1902).

Barthes, Roland, 'Le Nom d'Aziyadé', *Critique*, 28 (1972) pp. 104–17.

Beauvoir, Simone de, *The Second Sex*, trs. H. M. Parshley (New York: Alfred A. Knopf, 1953).

Benedict, Ruth, *The Chrysanthemum and the Sword* (Boston, Mass.: Houghton Mifflin, 1946).

Blanch, Lesley, 'Loti-land', *Cornhill Magazine*, 5, no. 168 (1956) pp. 388–404.

——, *Pierre Loti: The Legendary Romantic* (New York: Harcourt Brace Jovanovich, 1983).

Borgaud, Henri, 'Julien Viaud et son pseudonyme Pierre Loti', *Cahiers Pierre Loti*, November 1958, pp. 29–30.

Briquet, Pierre, *Pierre Loti et l'Orient* (Neuchâtel: Editions de la Braconnière, n.d.).

Brodin, Pierre, 'Should We Forget Pierre Loti?', *American Society Legion of Honor Magazine*, 33 (1962) pp. 97–104.

Bury, J. P. T., *France, 1814–1940* (New York: A. S. Barnes, 1962).

Calverley, E. E., *Islam: An Introduction*, vol. I (Cairo: American University at Cairo, 1958).

Clément, Cathérine, and Hélène Cixous, *La Jeune née* (Paris: Union Générale d'Editions, 1975).

Coleman, James S. (ed.), *Education and Political Development* (Princeton, N.J.: Princeton University Press, 1965).

Cooper, Elizabeth, *The Harim and the Purdah* (New York: Century, n.d.).

Dengler, Ian C., 'Turkish Women in the Ottoman Empire', in Lois Beck and Nikki Keddie (eds), *Women in the Muslim World* (Cambridge, Mass.: Harvard University Press, 1978) pp. 229–44.

Duplessy, Lucien, 'Pierre Loti a-t-il fait des romans?', *Grande Revue*, December 1925, pp. 219–40.

Edib, Halide, *Turkey Faces West* (New Haven, Conn.: Yale University Press, 1930).

El Saadawi, Nawal, *The Hidden Face of Eve*, trs. and ed. Sherif Hetata (London: Zed Press, 1980).

Ellis, William, *Polynesian Researches: Society Islands, Tutuai Islands, and New Zealand* (Rutland, Vt: Charles E. Tuttle, 1969).

Fallah-Najmeh, Thérèse, 'La Femme musulmane vue par Pierre Loti' (Thèse pour le doctorat de 3ᵉ cycle, Université de Paris IV, 1975).

Fanoudh-Siefer, Léon, *Le Mythe du nègre et de l'Afrique noire dans la littérature française* (Paris: Librairie C. Klincksieck, 1968).

Faust, Allen K., *The New Japanese Womanhood* (New York: George Doran, 1926).

La Femme au XIXe siècle (Lyon: Presses Universitaires de Lyon, n.d.).

Fernea, Elizabeth Warnock and Basima Qattan Bezirgan (eds), *Middle Eastern Muslim Women Speak* (Austin, Tx.: University of Texas Press, 1977).

Fetterley, Judith, *The Resisting Reader* (Bloomington, Ind.: Indiana University Press, 1977).

Flottes, Pierre, *Le Drame intérieur de Pierre Loti* (Paris: Le Courrier Littéraire, 1937).

Freud, Sigmund, *Collected Papers*, 3rd edn, vol. III, trs. Alix and James Strachey (London: Hogarth Press, 1946).

——, *The Complete Psychological Works*, trs. and ed. James Strachey in collaboration with Anna Freud (London: Hogarth Press and Institute of Psychoanalysis, 1957).

Fryer, Judith, *The Faces of Eve: Women in the Nineteenth-Century American Novel* (New York: Oxford University Press, 1976).

Funakoa, Suetoshi, '"Le Journal de Nagasaki" et *Mme Chrysanthème* de Pierre Loti', *Etudes de langue et littérature françaises*, XXX (1977) pp. 68–92.

Garnett, Lucy, *Turkey of the Ottomans* (New York: Charles Scribner's Sons, 1911).

Gilbert, Sandra M., and Susan Gubar, *The Madwoman in the Attic: The Woman Writer and the Nineteenth-Century Literary Imagination* (New Haven, Conn.: Yale University Press, 1979).

Gubar, Susan, '"The Blank Page" and the Issues of Female Creativity', in Elizabeth Abel (ed.), *Writing and Sexual Difference* (Chicago: University of Chicago Press, 1982) pp. 73–93.

Guillaume, Alfred, *Islam* (Harmondsworth, Middx: Penguin Books, 1962).

Hacioglu, Necdet, 'La Turquie vue par Pierre Loti' (dissertation, Université de Poitiers, 1978).

Haim, Sylvia G., 'The Arab Woman in the Mirror of Literature', *Middle East Studies*, 17, no. 4 (October 1981) pp. 515–20.

Hargreaves, Alex, *The Colonial Experience in French Fiction* (London: Macmillan, 1982).

Hays, H. R., *The Dangerous Sex: The Myth of Feminine Evil* (New York: G. P. Putnam's Sons, 1964).

Hearn, Lafcadio, *Japan: An Interpretation* (New York: Grosset & Dunlap, 1904).

Hélys, Marc, *L'Envers d'un roman: le secret des Désenchantées* (Paris: Perrin, 1923).

Horney, Karen, *Feminine Psychology* (New York: W. W. Norton, 1967).

——, *New Ways in Psychoanalysis* (New York: W. W. Norton, 1939).

Irigaray, Luce, 'Ce sexe qui n'en est pas un', in Elaine Marks and Isabelle de Courtivron (eds), *New French Feminisms: An Anthology* (Amherst, Mass.: University of Massachusetts Press, 1980).

James, Henry, *Essays in London and Elsewhere* (New York: Harper, 1893).

Johnson, Robert Brown, 'A Reexamination and Revaluation of the Dual Nature in the Life and Work of Pierre Loti' (dissertation, University of Wisconsin, 1949).

Jourda, Pierre, *L'Exotisme dans la littérature française*, I, *Le Romantisme* (Geneva: Slatkine Reprints, 1970).

Lebel, Roland, *Histoire de la littérature coloniale en France* (Paris: Librairie Larose, 1931).

Lebra, Joyce, Joy Paulson and Elizabeth Powers (eds), *Women in Changing Japan* (Boulder, Colo.: Westview Press, 1976).

Lefêvre, Raymonde, *La Vie inquiète de Pierre Loti* (Paris: Société Française d'Editions Littéraires et Techniques, 1934).

——, *Les Désenchantées de Pierre Loti* (Paris: Société Française d'Editions Littéraires et Techniques, 1939).

Legrand, Jacques, 'Clefs pour Les Désenchantées', *Cahiers Pierre Loti*, no. 68 (December 1968) pp. 21–32.

Leguillon, Rolande, 'Un aspect de l'amour chez Pierre Loti', *Rice University Studies*, 59, no. 3 (1973) pp. 43–53.

Lerner, Michael G., *Pierre Loti* (New York: Twayne Publishers, 1974).

Lewis, Bernard, 'The Question of Orientalism', *The New York Review of Books*, 29, no. 11 (June 1982) pp. 49–56.

Lloyd, P. C., *Africa in Social Change* (Baltimore, Md.: Penguin Books, 1967).

McMillan, James, *Housewife or Harlot* (New York: St Martin's Press, 1981).

Maurin, Mario, 'Pierre Loti et les voies du sacré', *Modern Language Notes*, 81, no. 3 (May 1966) pp. 297–307.

Mears, Eliot Grinnell, *Modern Turkey* (New York: Macmillan, 1924).

Millett, Kate, *Sexual Politics* (New York: Doubleday, 1970).

Millward, Keith G., *L'Oeuvre de Pierre Loti et l'esprit fin de siècle* (Paris: Librairies Nizet, 1955).

Mora, Gabriela, and Karen S. Van Hooft (eds), *Theory and Practice of Feminist Literary Criticism* (Ypsilanti, Mich.: Bilingual Press, 1982).

Newbury, Colin, *Tahiti Nui: Change and Survival in French Polynesia, 1767–1945* (Honolulu: University Press of Hawaii, 1980).

Nishimoto, Koji, 'Loti en face du Japon', *Revue de l'Université Laval*, v, 16 (1962) pp. 433–48.

Njoko, John E. Eberegbkulum, *The World of the African Woman* (Metuchen, N.J.: Scarecrow Press, 1980).

Oliver, Douglas L., *Ancient Tahitian Society* (Honolulu: University Press of Hawaii, 1974).

Ovesey, Lionel, 'The Homosexual Conflict', *Psychiatry*, 19 (1954) pp. 243–50.

Passin, Herbert, 'Japan', in James S. Coleman (ed.), *Education and Political Development* (Princeton, N.J.: Princeton University Press, 1965).

——, *Society and Education in Japan*, Comparative Education Series, Comparative Education Studies (New York: Columbia University Press, 1965).

Paulme, Denise, *Women of Tropical Africa*, ed. and trs. H. M. Wright (Berkeley, Cal.: University of California Press, 1963).

Paulson, Joy, 'Evolution of the Feminine Ideal', in Joyce Lebra, Joy Paulson and Elizabeth Powers (eds), *Women in Changing Japan* (Boulder, Colo.: Westview Press, 1976).

Poulet, Robert, 'Pierre Loti enchanteur désenchanté', *Le Spectacle du monde*, January 1975, pp. 66–71.

Praz, Mario, *The Romantic Agony*, trs. Angus Davidson, 2nd edn (Oxford: Oxford University Press, 1979).

Rafter, Basil, *La Femme dans l'oeuvre de Pierre Loti* (Paris: Presses Universitaires de France, 1938).

Richards, Alexis J., 'Exoticism in the Works of Pierre Loti' (dissertation, State University of Iowa, 1949).

Roheim, Géza, 'The Evolution of Culture', *International Journal of Psychoanalysis*, 15 (1934) pp. 387–418.

Sacré-Coeur, Soeur Marie André du, *La Femme noire en Afrique occidentale* (Paris: Payot, 1939).

Said, Edward, *Orientalism* (New York: Vintage Books, 1979).

Schwab, Raymond, *La Renaissance orientale* (Paris: Payot, 1950).

Schwartz, William, *The Imaginative Interpretation of the Far East in Modern French Literature* (Paris: Librairie Ancienne Honoré Champion, 1927).

Scribner, Helen, *Pierre Loti vu à travers son oeuvre* (Poitiers: Société Française d'Imprimerie, 1932).

Serban, N., *Pierre Loti: sa vie et son oeuvre* (Paris: Presses Françaises, 1924).

Showalter, Elaine, *A Literature of their Own: British Women Novelists from Brontë to Lessing* (Princeton, N.J.: Princeton University Press, 1977).

Siefert, Susan, *The Dilemma of the Talented Heroine: A Study in Nineteenth-Century Fiction* (Montreal: Eden Press, 1977).

Singer, Erwin, *Key Concepts in Psychotherapy* (New York: Basic Books, 1965).

Skinner, Cornelia Otis, *Madame Sarah* (Boston, Mass.: Houghton Mifflin, 1967).

Smith, Robertson W., *Kinship and Marriage in Early Arabia* (London: A. & C. Black, 1903; re-issued by Boston, Mass.: Beacon Press, n.d.).

Stanton, Theodore (ed.), *The Woman Question in Europe* (New York: G. P. Putnam's Sons, 1884).

Strem, George, 'Un chercheur d'âme, Pierre Loti', *La Revue de l'Université Laval* (Quebec), 14, no. 9 (1960) pp. 780–893.

Szyliowicz, Irene L., 'The Role of Stamboul in Pierre Loti's Turkish Fiction', *Turkish Studies Association Bulletin*, VII, no. 2 (1983) pp. 1–5.

Taboulet, G., and J. C. Demariaux, *La Vie dramatique de Gustave Viaud* (n.p.: Edition du Scorpion, 1963).

Taha-Hussein, Moenis, *Le Romantisme français et l'Islam* (Beirut, Lebanon: Dar al-Maarif, 1962).

Taşkiran, Tezer, *Women in Turkey*, trs. Nida Tektaş, ed. Anna G. Edmonds (Istanbul: Redhouse Yayinevi, 1976).

Tieghem, Paul van, *Le Romantism dans la littérature européenne* (Paris: Editions Albin Michel, 1948).

Traz, Robert, *Pierre Loti* (Paris: Librairie Hachette, 1948).

Vaka, Demetra, *Haremlik* (Boston, Mass.: Houghton Mifflin, 1909).

Valence, Odette, and Samuel Loti-Viaud, *La Famille de Pierre Loti ou l'éducation passionnée* (Paris: Calmann-Lévy, 1940).

Wake, Clive, *The Novels of Pierre Loti* (The Hague: Mouton, 1974).

Weir, A. L., 'Two Views of Exoticism: the Indias of E. M. Forster and Pierre Loti', *Exploration*, 7 (1979) pp. 17–28.

Zeldin, Theodore, *France 1848–1945*, vol. I: *Ambition, Love, and Politics* (Oxford: Clarendon Press, 1973).

Works and Articles Consulted

Abadan-Unat, Nermin, *Women in Turkish Society* (Leiden: E. J. Brill, 1981).

Abel, Elizabeth (ed.), *Writing and Sexual Difference* (Chicago: University of Chicago Press, 1982).

Accad, Evelyne, *Veil of Shame: The Role of Women in the Contemporary Fiction of North Africa and the Arab World* (Sherbrooke, Canada: Editions Naaman, 1978).

Adam, Juliette, *My Literary Life* (New York: D. Appleton, 1904).

——, *The Romance of my Childhood and Youth* (New York: D. Appleton, 1902).

Adams, Henry *Tahiti*, ed. Robert E. Spiller (New York: Scholars' Facsimiles and Reprints, 1947).

Atabinen, Rechid Saffet, *Pierre Loti: héroique ami des turques* (Istanbul: Association culturelle Franco-Turque, 1950).

Babbitt, Irving, *Rousseau and Romanticism* (Boston, Mass.: Houghton Mifflin, 1979).

Beck, Lois, and Nikki Keddie, *Women in the Muslim World* (Cambridge, Mass.: Harvard University Press, 1978).

Bernhardt, Sarah, *Mémoires de Sarah Berhardt: ma double vie* (Paris: Librairie Charpentier et Fasquelle, 1907).

Bird, C. W., *Pierre Loti: correspondant et dessinateur, 1872–1889* (Paris: Impressions Pierre André, 1947).

——, 'The Origin of the Name "Rarahu"', *Modern Language Notes*, February 1946, p. 120.

Blanchot, Maurice, *The Siren's Song*, trs. Sacha Rabinovitch, ed. Gabriel Jasipovici (Bloomington, Ind.: Indiana University Press, 1982).

Borie, Jean, *Le Tyran timide; le naturalisme de la femme au XIXᵉ siècle* (Paris: Editions Klincksieck, 1973).

Branca, Patricia, *Silent Sisterhood* (London: Croom Helm, 1975).

Brown, Cheryl L., and Karen Olsen (eds), *Feminist Criticism: Essays on Theory, Poetry, and Prose* (Metuchen, N.J.: Scarecrow Press, 1978).

Broyard, Anatole, review of Peter Gray, *The Bourgeois Experience: Victoria to Freud*, vol. I. *Education of the Senses*, in *New York Times*, 29 December 1983, p. C18.

Bullough, Vern L., and Bonnie Bullough, *The Subordinate Sex* (Urbana, Ill.: University of Illinois Press, 1973).

Busson, T. W., 'Pierre Loti and the *Roman d'un spahi*', *South Atlantic Quarterly*, 26 (1927) pp. 40–9.

Cario, Louis, 'Pierre Loti aux Armées', *Mercure de France*, July 1923, pp. 97–110.

Colmant, Paul, 'Pierre Loti: douleur d'une mère', *Etudes Classiques*, 28 (1960) pp. 312–16.

Comillon, Susan Koppelman (ed.), *Images of Women in Fiction: Feminist Perspectives* (Bowling Green, Ohio: Bowling Green University Popular Press, 1972).

Courrèges, Michel, 'Les Pouvoirs de la femme', *Cahiers du Sud*, no. 292 (n.d.) pp. 419–27.

Culler, Jonathan, *On Deconstruction: Theory and Criticism after Structuralism* (Ithaca, N.Y.: Cornell University Press, 1982).

Cunningham, Gail, *The New Woman and the Victorian Novel* (New York: Barnes & Noble, 1978).

Daudet, Léon, *Souvenir des milieux littéraires, politiques, artistiques et médicaux*, I (Paris, 1920).

D'Auvergne, Edmund B., *Pierre Loti: The Romance of a Great Writer* (Port Washington, N. Y.: Kennikat Press, 1970).

Delamont, Sara, and Loran Duffin, *The Nineteenth-Century Woman: Her Cultural and Physical World* (New York: Barnes & Noble, 1978).

Desrieux, V. Jean, 'Loti intime, impressions et souvenirs', *Le Correspondant*, 5, no. 303 (1926) pp. 524–35.

Dinnerstein, Dorothy, *The Mermaid and the Minotaur* (New York: Harper Row, 1976).

Dubois, Jacques, 'Pierre Loti aujourd'hui', *Revue des Sciences Humaines*, 117 (1965) pp. 81–92.

Ellman, Mary, *Thinking about Women* (New York: Harcourt, Brace and World, 1968).

El Nouty, Hassan, *Le Proche-Orient dans la littérature française de Nerval à Barrès* (Paris: Librairie Nizet, 1958).

Estève, Louis, *L'Hérédité romantique dans la littérature contemporaine* (Paris: Gastein Serge, 1914).

Felman, Shoshana, 'Rereading Femininity', *Yale French Studies*, no. 62 (1981) pp. 19–44.

Freud, Sigmund, *Collected Papers*, trs. Joan Riviere, 4th edn, 2 vols (London: Hogarth Press, 1946).

Furst, L. R., *Romanticism in Perspective* (New York: Humanities Press, 1970).

Gille, Philippe, *La Bataille littéraire* (Paris: V. Havard, 1891).

Giraud, Victor, 'La Jeunesse de Pierre Loti', *Revue des Deux Mondes*, June 1926, pp. 698–709.

Gutton, Francis, *Le Souvenir de Pierre Loti en Turquie* (n.p.: Les Amis de Loti, 1934).

Hagstrom, Jean H., *Sex and Sensibility* (Chicago, Ill.: University of Chicago Press, 1980).

Hamilton, Roberta, *The Liberation of Women* (London: Allen & Unwin, 1978).

Heilbrun, Carolyn, *Toward a Recognition of Androgyny* (New York: Alfred A. Knopf, 1973).

——, *Reinventing Womanhood* (New York: W. W. Norton, 1979).

Hélys, Marc, 'Pierro Loti, mon beau souvenir', *Le Figaro*, 10 June 1933, p. 5.

Hirschfeld, Magnus, *Die Travestiten, eine Untersuchung über den erotischen Verkleidungstrieb* (Berlin: n.p., 1910).

Jardine, Alice, 'Gynesis', *Diacritics*, 12, no. 2 (Summer 1982) pp. 54–65.

Javadi, Hasan, 'Persian Literary Influence on English Literature' (dissertation, University of California, Berkeley, 1979).

Johnson, Barbara, *The Critical Difference* (Baltimore, Md.: Johns Hopkins University Press, 1980).

Kennard, Jean, *Victims of Convention* (Hamden, Conn.: Archon Books, 1978).

——, *New Literary History*, 13, no. 1 (1981) pp. 69–88.

Kolbenschlag, Madonna, *Kiss Sleeping Beauty Good-bye: Breaking the Spell of Feminine Myths and Models* (New York: Doubleday, 1979).

Kolodny, Annette, 'Dancing Through the Minefield: Some Observations on the Theory, Practice, and Politics of a Feminist Literary Criticism', *Feminist Studies*, 6, no. 1 (Spring 1980) pp. 1–22.

——, 'A Map for Rereading: On Gender and the Interpretation of Literary Texts', *New Literary History*, 11, no. 3 (Spring 1980) pp. 451–67.

——, ' "The Panther Captivity" ', *Critical Inquiry*, 8, no. 8 (Winter 1981) pp. 329–45.

La Rochefoucauld, Gabriel de, *Constantinople avec Loti* (Paris: Editions de France, 1928).

Lefêvre, Raymonde, *Le Mariage de Loti* (Paris: Société Française d'Editions Littéraires et Techniques, 1935).

Leguillon, Rolande, 'Une Réévaluation de l'oeuvre de Pierre Loti', *Cahiers Pierre Loti*, no. 56 (1970) pp. 20–8.

Lemaire, Michel, *Le Dandysme de Baudelaire à Mallarmé* (Montreal: Presses de l'Université de Montréal, 1978).

Lerner, Michael, review of Clive Wake, *The Novels of Pierre Loti*, in *Lettres Romanes*, May 1976, pp. 180–3.

——, 'Pierre Loti as Dramatist: *Judith Renaudin*', *Nottingham French Studies*, 13 (1974) pp. 61–72.

Lunel, Armand, 'Les Amours de Pierre Loti au Sénégal', *Cahiers Pierre Loti*, March 1958, pp. 12–16.

Lewis, Raphaela, *Everyday Life in Ottoman Turkey* (New York: G. P. Putnam's Sons, 1971).

Mabbott, Thomas Olive, 'Correspondence', *Modern Language Notes*, 61, no. 5 (1946) p. 288.

Mallet, Frederic, *Pierre Loti: son oeuvre* (Paris: La Nouvelle Revue Critique, 1923).

Marks, Elaine, 'Women and Literature in France', *Signs*, 3 (Summer 1978) pp. 832–42.

Maurice, René, *En Marge d'Aziyadé* (Paris: Editions Universelles, 1945).

Mc C. Pastner, Carroll, 'Englishmen in Arabia: Encounters with Middle Eastern Women', *Signs*, Winter 1978, pp. 309–23.

Miller, Nancy K., 'Emphasis Added: Plots and Plausibilities in Women's Fiction', *PMLA*, 96 (1981) pp. 36–48.

Minai, Naila, *Women in Islam: Tradition and Transition in the Middle East* (New York: Seaview Books, 1981).

Nishimoto, Koji, 'Loti en face du Japon', *Revue de l'Université Laval* (Quebec), 5, no. 15 (1961) pp. 337–50.

Patai, Raphael (ed.), *Women in the Modern World* (New York: Free Press, 1967).

Pearson, Carol, and Katherine Pope, *The Female Hero in American and British Literature* (New York: R. R. Bowler, 1981).

Peyre, Henri, *What is Romanticism?* (Birmingham, Ala.: University of Alabama Press, 1977).

Poucel, Victor, 'Loti l'amour, la mort', *Etudes*, October–November 1923, pp. 129–45.

Ridge, George, *The Hero in French Romantic Literature* (Athens, Ga.: University of Georgia Press, 1959).

Sandison, Alan, *The Wheel of Empire* (New York: St Martin's Press, 1967).

Sherman, Julia A., and Evelyn T. Beck (eds), *The Prism of Sex* (Madison, Wis.: University of Wisconsin Press, 1977).

Showalter, Elaine, 'Feminine Criticism in the Wilderness', *Critical Inquiry*, 8, no. 2 (Winter 1981) pp. 179–205.

Singer, June, *Androgyny* (New York: Archon Press, 1976).

Skura, Meredith Anne, *The Literary Use of the Psychoanalytic Process* (New Haven, Conn.: Yale University Press, 1981).

Smith, Bonnie G., *Ladies of the Leisure Class: The Bourgeoises of Northern France in the Nineteenth Century* (Princeton, N.J.: Princeton University Press, 1981).

Smith, Jane I. (ed.), *Women in Contemporary Muslim Societies* (Lewisburg, Penn.: Bucknell University Press, 1980).

Strem, George, 'Un Chercheur d'âme, Pierre Loti', *Revue de l'Université Laval, Québec*, 15, no. 1 (1960) pp. 65–77.

Stubbs, Patricia, *Women and Fiction: Feminism and the Novel, 1880–1920* (New York: Barnes & Noble, 1929).

Thomas, William I., 'The Mind of Woman and the Lower Races', in Thomas F. Pettigrew (ed.), *The Sociology of Race Relations* (New York: Free Press, 1980).

Ugurel, Refia, *L'Education de la femme en Turquie* (Geneva: Georg, n.d.).

van Tieghem, Paul, *Le Romantisme dans la littérature européenne* (Paris: Editions Albin Michel, 1948).

Waardenburg, Jean-Jacques, *L'Islam dans le miroir de l'occident* (Paris: Mouton, 1962).

Waddy, Charis, *Women in Muslin History* (London: Longman, 1980).

Wagner, Geoffrey, *Five for Freedom* (London: George Allen & Unwin, 1972).

Woolf, Virginia, *A Room of One's Own* (New York: Harcourt Brace Jovanovich, 1929).

Zeyneb Hanoum, *A Turkish Woman's European Impressions* (London: Seeley Service, 1913).

Index

References to the Notes on pp. 122–52 are expressed as the page number followed by the note number in parenthesis.